Holly Caster

All
About
Eve

More About All About Eve

More About

 Random House, New York

All About Eve

a colloquy by Gary Carey with

Joseph L. Mankiewicz

together with his screenplay

All About Eve

Library of Congress Catalog Card Number: 72-2742

ISBN: 0-394-48248-4

Manufactured in the United States of America by Haddon Craftsmen, Scranton, Pa.

97532468

First Printing

With my love, for:
(in order of appearance)

Rosemary

Alexandra Kate

More About All About Eve

More About

All About Eve

a colloquy by Gary Carey with

Joseph L. Mankiewicz

To get to Joseph L. Mankiewicz' home in Pound Ridge, New York, nondrivers take the Harlem-Central Line from Grand Central Station to the Mt. Kisco stop. That first day I went to visit Mankiewicz was dreary with rain; the train's windows were dirty and cracked; there was too much heat; and the seats were so arranged that everyone had to ride facing backwards. The unsavory background further unsettled my already anxious mind. I was worried that the train would be late and that the tape recorder wouldn't work (it didn't), and I was frankly apprehensive about meeting Mankiewicz. He has a distaste for interviews in general — and, in particular, for interviewers who paraphrase what he has to say and then quote him directly in language which is not his own.

(He recalls with particular dismay an extensive one he granted the French magazine *Cahiers du Cinema*. I later discovered that this interview, originally published in the French edition, had been given in English, translated into French, and then, for the American edition, retranslated from the French into a pidgin English which lost all of the director's conversational flavor, distorted most of his meaning, and resulted in what he describes as "incoherent gibberish. Shrdlu, in fact.")

As I looked over the Harlem-Central timetable, I noticed that the final stop was Brewster, which in *All About Eve* is the locale of Lloyd Richards' "little place just two hours from New York."* Consequently, this might have been

* The Brewster station was also the opening vista of *A Letter to Three Wives*, establishing the suburb with "those horrible chain stores that breed like rabbits."

(particularly from the look of it) the very train Margo missed that eventful night Karen drained the Richards' coupe of its gas. I was visiting Mankiewicz to find out all about *All About Eve* from genesis to *fait accompli,* and being superstitious, I regarded this mental double exposure of Margo and me on the same train as some kind of good omen.

The train pulled into Mt. Kisco only about five minutes late and Mankiewicz was waiting to meet me at the station; a stocky man with an open, friendly face who looks a good deal younger than his years. He has the gift of putting people immediately at their ease; as we drove from the station to Pound Ridge (about a twenty-minute drive), the conversation was relaxed, and although it served the purpose of feeling each other out, there was nothing tentative about it. I was to find out that "tentative" was applicable to almost nothing about him.

When we reached the driveway of his home, Mankiewicz stopped the car to fetch an enormous stack of manuscripts, books, and letters from his mailbox. Never a notably prolific director, Mankiewicz has made only three films in the past ten years. Much of that unproductive time he rather bluntly attributes to a deliberate and depressed withdrawal from creative activity due to the brutalization by its releasing company of *Cleopatra,* a film which Mankiewicz rarely refers to by name and has deleted from any filmography of his work over which he has control. Still, judging from the pile of letters to be answered, scripts and books submitted for his approval, his current disenchantment does not seem to be regarded as irrevocable. (Nor is it; Mankiewicz has his plans for the future, although they do not presently include writing for the screen. The only directorial project he speculated about, probably because it was the one least likely to come

6

to fruition, was a film version of *Macbeth* which would star Marlon Brando and Maggie Smith.)

The Mankiewicz home is a former dairy farm, an unpretentious and charming conglomerate of tiny white buildings, rolling fields, and duck ponds. Mankiewicz beeped the horn as we drove past the small main house, but did not come to a halt until we reached what had formerly been a cow barn, now converted into a study-workroom. The conversion had been done with taste: white plaster walls, beamed ceilings, and an imposing, rough-hewn stone fireplace. Four Oscars, an award from the New York Film Critics, diplomas, scrolls, and figurines from England, France, Italy, Japan, even Cuba — from "those organizations which proliferate all over the world, smugly designating the best of everything" — covered the mantel and walls. Nonetheless, there was none of the vainglorious ambience which overruns a prizewinner's trophy room. This was a warm and friendly workshop, lined with bookshelves whose contents showed a wide diversity of interests, all of which were extensively covered — and the books had obviously been read.

After lunch, provided by his attractive wife, Rosemary — described by Mankiewicz as "possibly the only Englishwoman with an awareness that coffee is more than just any brown liquid, heated" — we discussed how to proceed on this account of the making of *All About Eve*. A process which Mankiewicz described as "having, somehow, the flavor of a posthumous undertaking." I suggested that we work chronologically, which I presumed started with his coming upon Mary Orr's short story, "The Wisdom of Eve," the basis for the film. Mankiewicz attempted to oblige, starting at the point I had given him, but to ask Mankiewicz to start at a chronological point is to ask him to flash back. The flashback is to him not at all a device; it is "an omnipresent part of 'now' in time — that part of the past which is in everybody's present." So, with a quick cut, we were deep in Mankiewicz' past. (We were to remain in Mankiewicz' past for our next two meetings, and he was to linger even longer as he subsequently reworked and expanded upon those portions of the interview which quote him directly.)

It all really began with Mankiewicz' lifelong dedication — "a calling, really," in his words — as a theatre buff. Particularly, his almost obsessive interest in the "inhabitants of the theatre — those who cause it to exist — its creative commune." This affection is readily apparent from his library. Two entire walls of his study are lined with theatrical books: biographies, more biographies, encyclopedias, yearbooks, an extremely comprehensive collection of published plays from Aeschylus to Albee. But even without this ambience, one would sense it from the added warmth and fervor in Mankiewicz' voice whenever the conversation turns (as it invariably does) to the subject of the actor, his craft, "the quirks and frailties, the needs and talents of the performing personality." Once, after tuning up to the subject for ten minutes or so, Mankiewicz concluded: "I often wonder why serious students of the human psyche look to anything *but* theatre-folk for most of the answers they seek."

The genesis of *Eve* lay in this enduring fascination. "I imagine it surfaced for the first time," Mankiewicz said, "when I was about eight years old. I saw my first film — I think it was my first — in a lower Second Avenue movie theatre; could it have been called The Casino? Anyway, the film — which was entitled *Hock The Hun* or *Hock The*

8

Kaiser, that should date it — starred Jane and Catherine Lee. Two little girl actresses, precursors of Shirley Temple, who — apparently to this day — nobody but me has ever heard of. The movie was a First World War two-reel comedy in which these two little American girl spies were hiding from the Germans and a bee was about to sting one of them on her bare bottom — and betray their whereabouts to the brutal Huns. The suspense nearly destroyed me. But — most importantly — I remember that after the film was over I got up, walked down to the screen, and insisted upon looking behind it. I was convinced the two little girls would be there. I have never, since that day, been completely certain that actresses on the screen were altogether unreal — or that, off the screen, they were altogether real."

This inquisitiveness never waned, although his professional and personal proximity to theatre folk in his later life would seem to have been more than sufficient to engender both disillusionment and satiety. Mankiewicz had begun his career at Paramount Studios in 1929 as a title-writer (for "talking pictures," which were being released in the thousands of theatres still without equipment for sound projection), graduating to writing comedy scripts for Jack Oakie and W. C. Fields (including his original screenplay for the memorable *Million Dollar Legs* — and four episodes for the equally famous *If I Had a Million,* in one of which he created for Fields the "My Little Chickadee," "My Little Tomtit," etc., syndrome that Fields continued to utilize in later films). In 1931, at the age of twenty-two, he received his first Academy Award nomination, for the screenplay of *Skippy.*

In the mid-1930's he moved to MGM, where he first wrote *Manhattan Melodrama* — a Gable-Powell-Loy film "most noteworthy for having lured John Dillinger to his entrapment and death at the hands of the FBI." This was followed by two screenplays for Joan Crawford, *Forsaking all Others* and *I Live my Life* — successfully typical of the "madcap-young-heiress and brash-young-reporter film cycle of that Hollywood era." Then, refused an opportunity to direct by Louis B. Mayer, he was cajoled by that same "Great Cajoler" into a lengthy period of producing films for MGM's vast stable of female stars — innumerable vehicles for Miss Crawford, Margaret Sullavan, Katharine Hepburn, Myrna Loy, and Rosalind Russell, among others — a period he refers to as his "black years." His writing, which he contributed liberally to most of his productions, went uncredited due to the stringent regulations of the Screen Writers Guild (of which Mankiewicz had been a founding member and officer a few years earlier) — and he loathed having his creative identity restricted to that of "producer." (He still bridles at being referred to as a movie producer. Yet, among his productions at MGM were such vintage favorites as *Fury*, *The Philadelphia Story*, *Woman of the Year* and *Three Comrades*.)

In the early 1940's he moved to Twentieth Century-Fox, having been contractually granted the opportunity to direct. After writing (with Nunnally Johnson) and producing *The Keys of the Kingdom*, finally, in 1945, under the aegis of Ernst Lubitsch — who had been Mankiewicz' "friend, guide and preceptor" since his earliest junior-writer days at Paramount and of whom he still speaks with reverence — he directed his own screenplay of *Dragonwyck*. (Mankiewicz, by the way, dismisses as "utter fantasy" the scuttlebutt legend that he took over the direction from Lubitsch due to the latter's ill health. "For some time — ever since his heart attack during the shooting of *A Royal Scandal* — Ernst had not felt up to the physical demands of directing. Accordingly, he decided to function for a while only as a producer. Fox purchased the Anya Seton novel, *Dragonwyck*, for Lubitsch's production schedule — and he asked me to write the screenplay and direct it. Ernst is not credited on the screen — there is no producer's credit on *Dragonwyck* — but he did, in fact, produce it.")

By now, Mankiewicz' protean career had already spanned some fifteen years. "Hollywood, at the time," he commented, "was a small strangely remote enclave on the outskirts of Los Angeles — professionally and socially inbred and self-preoccupied — a weird mixture of goldmining camp and ivory ghetto. One knew almost everybody else casually and an ever-changing small group intimately. The major studios were separate duchies — and somehow one's contract implied an exclusivity not only of professional talents but of one's private and social life as well. By and large, those one worked with during the day became one's companions at night. Accordingly, during my ten years at MGM my Paramount friends, even my intimates, had inevitably grown remote. And now, as a subject or citizen (or serf, if you will) of Fox — there were new faces, new personalities, egos, and idiocies with which to cope and work and fraternize. Not different — mind you — just new."

During those first fifteen years, Mankiewicz had written and produced for, and was presently also directing, most of the current stars — the "great and near-great; the young not-to-be-denied; the aging scrambling-to-hold-on — and that vast mass who never quite fail but never quite succeed but who also never quit." The actor's persistent drive for success is, of course, an important theme of *All About Eve*. I asked him how he would define it. Mankiewicz pulled at his pipe:

"The definitive answer, I think, would be different for

each individual ego. But there are some basic common components. For one — what amounts to an obsessive need for the young actress/actor to acquire a substitute identity. A personality-proxy, really, wherewith she can attain acknowledgment, acceptance, even love and/or its many equivalents, from a society in which she is usually unable to function successfully as just herself. Or what she considers herself to be, or not to be — which is the same thing.

"For another — possibly an even more acutely obsessive need for the no-longer-young actress to ensure, at the very least, *survival* for that substitute identity which had for so long sustained her. To each and all of them, you know, there arrives that one last time when the make-up comes off — to stay off. Leaving him, leaving her — as what? With what?"

Mankiewicz grinned. "I have no intention of relating chapter and verse of *The Actor: The Origin And Continuing History Of The Species*. That's just one of the many books I've promised myself to write before my Exit into That Great Green Room Above — but which I most likely won't. Let me present to you, though, a valid capsulized concept of how the actor could have come to be — and how his place in society could have evolved . . . " He took another long drag on his pipe. He has been a pipe-smoker for forty-five years — smokes them unceasingly — about a pound of Barking Dog tobacco every ten days — and is inordinately proud of his ability to keep his pipe from going out.

"A minor talent — keeping my pipe lit — but one of my few remaining competitive social aptitudes. Back to the actor. It is my belief that, historically, the actor could have predated fire, the wheel, the axe, the priest — every major manifestation of human creativity, really — except possibly killing and making noise.

"Let's fade in, then — or 'iris in,' which is earlier — upon a particular occasion in the dim prehistory óf what we call, hopefully, *Homo sapiens*. One pleasant evening, herded together by the earliest stirrings of a gregarious instinct, a gathering of our forebears was sprawled listlessly on some sheltered slope, temporarily safe from attack by the many larger and stronger and more resourceful animals which customarily and casually ate them.

"They, our forebears, in turn, had just finished their own feeding — gorging themselves beyond saturation with whatever could be pulled from the earth or hit by a rock — already committed to probably one of the earliest and certainly most enduring of human rituals: The Evening Meal.

"And there they sat — then, as now. Bellies distended, eyes glazed by gluttony, acutely aware of visceral discomfort and mentally aware of nothing at all — the dreary silence broken only by an occasional belch or break-of-wind. Incapable of communication with each other — and, in any case, with nothing to communicate. Then, as now. Facing, with apathetic resignation, that most empty and most frightening time of the human day as *Homo sapiens* has created it for himself: the few hours that stretch endlessly between mankind's Evening Meal — and mankind's Bedtime.

"How indescribably intolerable they must have been, those evening hours during our earliest existence. With literally nothing to distract our forebears from the stultification of their — then, as now — spiritual emptiness and lack of resource. Incapable, yet, of conceiving the wheel much less TV and the movies, gin rummy, booze, pool, pot, pornography — some of the countless more or less successful distractions whereby we, the ultimate refinement of *Homo sapiens, can* make it from dinner to bed. Some of the time.

13

"But, on that particular pre-historic evening whereof I speak, something happened. Something that broke into the seemingly hopeless lethargy like a thunderclap — and changed the very nature of living for those stuffed witless human creatures. For suddenly one of them jumped to his feet (as I picture it, he'd been sitting off to one side, not really part of the pack, maybe smaller and weaker than the rest) smeared some birdshit over his face, shoved a big feather up his ass, and began to prance up and down waving his arms and making noises like a roc or some equivalent pre-historic chicken. And at that precise moment, my friend — Curtain Time, Make-up, Costume, and the Actor simultaneously came into being.

"The others stared at him for an instant; then intuitively roared with pleasure. The first Belly Laugh. They yelled for more — and got it, I'm sure. The first Encore. That poor bastard with the feather up his ass must have pranced and danced and cackled himself into total exhaustion that first First Night. When — we mustn't forget — the Audience, too, was born.

"But what also resulted from that particular occasion was — the nature of the actor's place in the Audience's world. Because the next night, as they sat around with their swollen bellies, they called for him to get up and do the same thing. Which he did, of course. Again and again, night after night — until, after a while, they stopped laughing at the chicken bit. They'd seen it too often. They went back to belching, scratching, yawning. So the actor got himself a fancier feather, maybe a bearskin or a dinosaur's tooth — maybe some other misfit came to him with a suggestion; but that's how Gag Men came to be, and that's a different story — and they laughed again. One time he hid behind a rock, imitated thunder or the roar of a lion, and frightened them. Thus he discovered the Audience liked to be afraid almost as much as to laugh — provided they knew it was make-believe. He was learning that every aspect of the Audience's world had its counterpart in a make-believe world which, it seemed, was the actor's private domain — and that revealing it was his private skill, his talent — and that this revelation, if successful, could ensure him acceptance within the tribe, within society.

"That may well have been why he shoved the feather up his ass in the first place. Possessed of the same, perhaps even greater, appetites and ambitions as the others, he had never before found a way — as *himself* — to attain that acceptance, let alone the share of leadership and adulation he craved. In terms of physical endowment, as I've postulated, he was probably ill-equipped (Did you know that Garrick, Booth, Kean, among many other greats, were under five feet six inches tall?) to compete in a very physical world. He was a lousy hunter, a pitiful warrior, given to daydreaming, pushed around or ignored, relegated to the remnants of food and least appetizing of the women, probably considered expendable in case of hostilities.

"But now — ever since that First Night — living was different for him. He now moved among his fellows with assurance, ate well, slept securely inside the cave — probably knocking off any number of tasty broads, in whose eyes he had suddenly acquired that strange special sexuality which women so often ascribe to men engaged in other than traditionally masculine pursuits. Why? Why that difference in his status when he *himself* was no different — when, by the reality-standards of the society in which he existed, he *himself* was every bit as insufficient as before?

"Simple. Because each evening, and maybe even on rainy afternoons, as *somebody or something else,* he had ministered to the basic need of that enduring human entity — the Mass Audience — to be beguiled and distracted when forced back upon its own inner resources which were — and are — nil. And that Mass Audience, in turn, had gratefully rewarded him for satisfying that desperate basic need with approval and applause. With a sense of belonging and having purpose within the tribe — with, at long last, an acceptance.

"Imagine. All that. Just for shoving a feather up your ass and making like a chicken. How infinitely more gratifying it must be today — how much more prideful, even ennobling — when that identity proxy can be Oedipus or Hamlet or Medea, St. Joan, Eliza Doolittle, Camille, even Auntie Mame. For that matter, even Margo Channing. Even *Eve.*"

While his intense preoccupation with "the theatre historically, and its inhabitants in terms of the inner 'alarums and excursions' which motivate them" never waned — and still hasn't — Mankiewicz, in 1949, wrote and directed the first of his manners-and-mores films, *A Letter to Three Wives,* which won for him the first two of his four successive Academy Awards for writing and direction. Mankiewicz has never had a personal press agent and he has never, as has become usual in the Oscar sweepstakes, indulged in any form of promotion in order to better his chances. Nor was he particularly shocked when he was informed by Darryl Zanuck himself that Twentieth Century-Fox had no intention of backing his film — that the studio was putting all of its advertising and publicity resources behind another nominee, *Twelve O'Clock High,* personally produced by Zanuck.

Mankiewicz, who enjoys referring to himself — as far as the realities of moviemaking are concerned — as "the oldest whore on the beat," took particular delight in winning his Oscars as an untouted dark horse. Even more, he became increasingly interested in 'The Award' itself, as a symbol. Or as he puts it:

" 'The Award' as also a totem. Its implications as a sort of cockamaimy immortality. Together with the conniving and soliciting and maneuvering that goes on for the acquisition of it — and, in the end, the strangely unenduring gratification it provides. Award-winning can often be followed, almost reactively, by a period of depression — not unlike suddenly going off amphetamines. Anyway, I found myself pondering these and other ramifications of 'The Award' syndrome; it would make an excellent frame, I thought, for a film — or play or book — about the theatre, the theatre-folk, those motivating 'alarums and excursions' I've been talking about."

The "pondering" was not a search for dramatic material; what Mankiewicz still needed was what Alfred Hitchcock has called "the McGuffin": the hook or gimmick upon which a plot hangs and by which it is triggered. This he came across in a short story, "The Wisdom of Eve," written by actress and sometime playwright Mary Orr.*

This story, which first appeared in *Cosmopolitan* in 1946 — some three years before it came to Mankiewicz' attention — is reportedly a lightly fictionalized account of an incident in the career of Elisabeth Bergner, the famous Austrian actress. "The Wisdom of Eve" concerns a stage-struck girl, Eve Harrington, who plays upon the sympathies of an aging and

* Miss Orr's greatest success as a playwright was *Wallflower*, a domestic comedy she wrote in collaboration with Reginald Denham in 1944. She also appeared in its original Broadway cast.

happily married Broadway actress Margola Cranston (sic), becomes her understudy, and then ruthlessly attempts to replace her both on stage and in her husband's affections. Though Eve fails in this attempt, she does win the lead in a new play written by Lloyd Richards, Margola's favorite playwright, and eventually steals Mr. Richards away from his wife Karen, also an actress, who happens to be Margola's best friend.

Miss Orr's story was little more than an anecdote, but it had the ring of true theatrical scuttlebutt as told out of school, and attracted enough attention to be adapted as a radio drama. At that time, however, the story departments of the major film companies were extremely diligent in their search for potential material, and "The Wisdom of Eve" came to the attention of James Fisher, then head of Twentieth Century-Fox's story department. As was standard procedure, Miss Orr's story was mimeographed and then sent to the studio's various contractual producers, writers, and directors.

Mankiewicz showed me the memo from Fisher which accompanied the story, suggesting that it was "something unusual" and adding as possible encouragement that the rights could be obtained at an extremely reasonable price. There is nothing about the memo to suggest that Fisher knew of Mankiewicz' interest in doing a theatrical film — it reads like a routine story department coverage. But the story hit home: it gave Mankiewicz the "McGuffin" he needed.

II

Mankiewicz began writing *All About Eve* (or *Best Performance*, as it was then called) in the early fall of 1949, in the peace and quiet of a ranch near Santa Barbara. The treatment* took three months to complete; the first rough draft of the screenplay, six weeks. The shooting script was delivered in mid-March. According to Twentieth Century-Fox's records, Mankiewicz' services as writer (for accounting purposes) terminated on March 24, 1950.

Anyone who has the opportunity to compare the original story with the subsequent treatment and screenplay will realize the extent to which Mankiewicz rewrote and re-characterized those characters who have counterparts in Miss Orr's story. Addison DeWitt, Bill Sampson, Birdie Coonan, Max Fabian, Miss Caswell, and Phoebe are entirely of Mankiewicz' creation.

But the greatest change from the original was wrought upon the character of the famous actress. In the story, Margola Cranston is happily married, and as Miss Orr has someone say of her: "If she ever sees forty-five again, I'll have my eyes lifted." Well past forty and happily married were exactly what Mankiewicz did *not* feel were characteristic of the actress he wanted to portray; actually, what he wanted to dramatize was:

"The trauma and terror with which so many of them approach *both* age forty *and* the transition from married actress to just married woman. The transition of their main performing arena from stage — to home. And the rapid narrowing of roles available, down to the ultimate two: wife and/or woman.

"Let me digress a moment to get a definition straight. I'm talking about *actresses* (and actors, too, of course, except they're men and infinitely luckier and less complicated and

* A treatment is technical jargon for an outline, usually sketchy, but which Mankiewicz invariably constructed in great detail before going into screenplay, in which the story is broken down into scenes, the dramatic continuity is constructed, and the characters are developed.

less intriguing — to me, at any rate) — women who, since almost their earliest awareness of themselves, have been *compelled* to act in order to *be*. I am *not* talking about that vast remaining spectrum of those who appear on stage or screen (some successfully, at times, for a time) with all the emotional involvement of trained seals playing cornet solos. To wit: the big-titted sex symbols, the city-type cowboys, the country-type shitkickers, the once-and-future stuntmen, the TV transplants, the New England tawny-types, the Bennington dropouts who invariably make the cover of *Life* — you can supply the names as well as I. No, Margo, *the actress*, was — and is — none of these. She was — and is — a woman whose need to act equates with her need to breathe. Who, when she isn't 'on' — just isn't, at all.

"Forty years of age. Four O. Give or take a year, the single most critical chronological milestone in the life of an actress. Look, I *knew* these women. I'd been in love with some — I'd worked with many of them. In the 1930's I'd watch them roll into Paramount and Metro at six thirty in the morning on their way to hairdressing and make-up. Drive in usually with the top down, their hair all blown by the wind, no lipstick, their own eyelashes, wearing anything from a poncho to a polo coat — and I'd think Percy Westmore should be arrested for so much as touching a powder puff to their loveliness. Well, by the late thirties they were driving with the top up. Then, in the forties, they started wearing scarfs — and, by 1950, large hats. The pancake was getting thicker, the make-up took longer, the cameramen started using specially built little banks of 'inkies' to iron out wee bags and sags.

"Fortyish. You know, there's an old cue that never fails to stimulate some bitchy theatrical wisecracks—just drop the name of the current fortyish actress who is having to decide for the first time whether to play the mother of a late teenager. The jokes may be funny, but don't laugh. It's a bitterly sad point of no return for an actress. It usually means that a wide range of stimulating and gratifying identity-proxies — particularly those that reflect and sustain the metaphor of youth — would, from now on, be inexorably unavailable to her. That the personality-aliases left for her to assume would now become inevitably character roles and — if she was unlucky enough to have to go on and on and on — caricatures. Four O. Fortyish. For the actress, a kind of professional menopause, really . . .

"Well, so we'd grown up together, my generation of them; they were pushing forty — and so was I. But I was a writer and director, just beginning to formulate what I wanted to write and what I wanted my films to be about. And, lucky me, even if I'd been an actor, a male. There was — and is — the theatrical rub. Women's Lib has quite a point to make here: about a society which can evolve and foster a set of standards by which, at roughly age forty, the female actress is required to forswear the public projection of romantic and/or sexual allure — while the male actor carries on blithely.

"Gary Cooper was 'getting the girl' (a felicitous phrase, equating the female with a vice-presidency, a touchdown, or maybe the clap) after he was sixty; Gable was sixty, or close to it, when Marilyn Monroe (in *The Misfits*) wanted into his bed. Wayne, Fonda, and Cary Grant are well into their sixties; Kirk Douglas, Mitchum, Lancaster are among those in the middle fifties — hell, even Paul Newman and Brando are on the other side of forty-five. It'd make a fascinating sociological study: why our American morality considers it indulgently 'G' for Cary Grant to make love to, say, Ali Mc-

Graw (in her twenties) and would react with 'X' outrage at Ryan O'Neal (in his twenties) bedding down with, say, Ava Gardner (in her late forties). Me, if I were O'Neal, I'd choose Gardner any time.

"But that's how the career crumbles with the female of the theatre-folk. And that was one of the facets of the actress I wanted to explore. With Margo, I complicated and compounded the problem by having her — at age forty — in love with Bill. I couldn't have given her a more threatening love object. For one thing, as a director, he worked in the same profession which had provided her with a lifelong sustenance — from which she was about to undergo the involuntary weaning I've described. Bill could, and would, go on forever in that profession; her share of its sustenance, however, would depend upon whatever he happened to bring home with him at night. Would that, that — shared ration — be enough? She'd had her own, all of it, for so long. She'd been, don't forget, the only angel on the head of the pin. Would she grow to resent being, as it were, on some sort of ego-sharing welfare program?

"Another curve I threw the poor woman was to make Bill eight years younger than she. I've told you about how theatre-folk have their own arithmetic; not a new but a very old math, indeed. Margo describes it in the screenplay: 'Bill's thirty-two. He looks thirty-two. He looked it five years ago, he'll look it twenty years from now. I hate men.' And, later, to Karen: 'Those (eight) years stretch as the years go on.'

"Most importantly, I guess, I wanted Margo to dramatize, if even briefly, my concept of the actor and his/her early flight into the 'identity-proxy' or 'personality-substitute' or 'ego-alias' or whatever the hell else I've dubbed it. His/her subsequent measure of success in coping with society behind the mask of that 'proxy-substitute-alias.' And then, inevitably with the actress, the traumatic reemergence of that inner *Self* she had decided so long ago was inadequate to attain even acceptance. An inner *Self* from which she had hidden behind those magical protean masks, or — as in the most tragic of instances — a *Self* she had never really known at all . . .

"When you're Judy Garland, say. And at age *three** you're shoved onto a stage into a spotlight to sing 'Jingle Bells.' And from that moment on, you're told and told and *told* by everyone — from audiences that cheer you in that spotlight when you sing, to a draconian mother who drills the unshakable conviction into you (you'll carry it with you until you die) — that *only* in that spotlight, singing as loud as you can (didn't Mummy have you billed as 'The Little Girl with the Leather Lungs'?), were you even acceptable to society, much less attractive in any way at all — how the hell can you possibly, for the rest of your life, know *who you really are?* And offstage, offscreen, with the spotlights and arc lights dark, when all through childhood and puberty you were never spared the acute awareness — in endless crowded studio conferences — that your waist was unusually high and your shoulders unusually rounded ('humped,' they were often called in your presence), and that *other* than your singing there was nothing about you that would merit a second glance or second thought from anyone — wouldn't that substitute-identity, the identity that existed only in a spotlight, become pretty goddamn important to you? Wouldn't it, in fact, become the one and only source of acceptance, of

---

* The screenplay places Margo's stage debut at age four when she entered, "stark naked," as a fairy in A *Midsummer Night's Dream*.

security and salvation, in a society which apparently considered you otherwise worthless?

"And with the passing years and accumulating fat and the deteriorating effect of the pills and drugs and booze that had somehow kept you going — kept you unaware, anesthetized as it were, in between spotlights — wouldn't the approaching finish, the approaching *blackout* of that spotlight-identity terrify you almost beyond reason, drive you to a despair of being capable even to go on existing without it? Roughly, that was Judy. She was the most terrible loss of them all, and probably the greatest of the talents lost that way. Not that the pattern of her tragedy was unique. Not by hundreds, maybe thousands. From the most celebrated to the most unwept of the unclaimed identity-unknowns . . .

"There was Marilyn, of course. The symptoms, the sources of infection were different, but the syndrome was the same. More mawkish horseshit has been intoned and written about how 'Hollywood destroyed Marilyn Monroe.' Her particular pattern of self-destruction had been completed long before she ever heard of Schwab's Drugstore. But the movies — and her sudden, staggering, inexplicable movie stardom — did shape the finish for her, and hurry it. And cushioned it, in my opinion — in a strange way made the end easier for her. With the fantastic miracle of her 'career' already a shambles ten years ago, can you imagine Marilyn Monroe today, alive — existing as what? Where? How? Think about it.

"There were so many, many others — variations, all of them, on one tragic theme. Just some that come to mind: Olive Thomas, Lupe Velez, Jeanne Eagles, Thelma Todd, Carole Landis — why draw up lists? I could fill your cassettes with them. Strange, though, isn't it, how few men come to mind? There were plenty, of course. As noted, however, they usually went on so much longer before they ran out of masks. John Gilbert, for one. James Murray — remember him in King Vidor's *The Crowd?* — reportedly drowned himself. Milton Sills — big star, as big in his day as Gable — drove his car off a cliff, it was said . . .

"Lou Tellegen's reputed finish was, if nothing else, the most pertinent I've ever encountered. He was another great star of the early days — played Essex to Sarah Bernhardt's Elizabeth, I believe — married to Geraldine Farrar and co-starred with her. Well, in the mid-thirties, Lou Tellegen committed suicide. Apparently they found him surrounded by his vast collection of scrapbooks, crammed with clippings of the only life he had found tolerable, innumerable three-sheets (small posters) of his innumerable triumphs, and countless photos of himself as all of his 'proxies.' He was nude. It was said he'd committed hara-kiri. Not by means of a samurai sword, but with a pair of gold scissors — engraved with his name — the same pair he'd used to trim all those clippings, doubtlessly. Pertinent, don't you agree?

"Back, once more, to Margo. To the nature and ramifications of the actor's original, inner Self (really the *ego*, in psychiatric terms; one doesn't dare refer to it as such because, in common usage, the word has acquired so many other irrelevant meanings). Margo wasn't any of the above, of course. Nor was *All About Eve* about them. They, poor souls, were — and are — from another part of the Garden. Damned even before sinning. And their punishment, when the time came, or comes — with the stripping of the masks — is a total absence of any *ego* at all. Literally, an inner vacuum. With which, obviously, even mere existence becomes impossible.

"No, Margo's problem wasn't a — say — a 'void' behind

that public identity which had for so long, with her permission and connivance, usurped her private identity. It was more: 'I wish I knew what the hell, after all these years of exile, my Self will turn out to be.' Putting it simplistically, of course. Margo could accept that Bill was in love with what the spotlight picked up. But when that spotlight turned off (and stayed off) how would Bill then feel about — *what?* She couldn't even guess. She knew only that it would be female — and eight years older than Bill. It wouldn't cook, surely, keep house or take second billing. Given to infantile tantrums, probably, for which there'd now be no ducking the responsibility. The angers would be hers — Margo's — no longer Medea's. It would be her bitchiness, now — not Becky Sharp's. She would be growing old — not Elizabeth the Queen.

"Not, I submit, the well-known, well-worn problem of the career woman playing tug of war with career and marriage. Not this one. 'I'm forty and maybe a bit more — I have had a highly successful and gratifying public identity which, since age four, has also functioned as my private identity, but which is not me — and when that public identity, that alias, ceases to exist, which will be any day now, I just don't know what the hell will be there in its place — and I love a man who, in turn, can love only the identity which I am about to lose because he has never known any other as me.' This is a very special problem, believe me. Indigenous to the female of the theatre-folk."

In creating Eve, Mankiewicz set out to portray a more universal type, a female whose ambitions and machinations are not uniquely indigenous to the theatre:

26

"There are Eves afoot in every competitive stratum of our society, wherever there's a top you can get to from the bottom. Eves are predatory animals; they'll prefer a terrain best suited to their marauding techniques, hopefully abundant with the particular plunder they're after. But in default of that happiest of hunting grounds — they'll work any beat at hand.

"Watch little girls. Certain little girls, that is. Eve's the one who always seems to wind up at the head of the line for cookies — she'll make or steal her own gold stars to take home if teacher can't be conned into giving her one — she'll throw fits, even run up fake fevers, if the prize is worth it to her. Eve is the one who must inevitably attain Daddy's assurance that he loves her more than he loves Mummy — and then goes after the identical assurance from Mummy.

"Full-grown, in the workaday world, Eve is everywhere. Corporations great and small, department stores, magazines and publishing houses, advertising companies, even — as in the script — breweries. Secretarial pools breed Eves like guppies.

"In the theatre, in the movies, in show business, she's there because there lies the particular loot she's after. 'Loot' may be an inaccurate word; it implies money. Of course there are hustler 'actresses' after money — but they, almost always, are after nothing else. And with no discernible talents out of the hay. They operate usually on the fringes of Broadway, TV, and the movies — drift back and forth to what used to be called Café Society and/or the Jet Set — but their true habitat and trade, however vaguely legitimatized by publicity puffs and multiple marriages, is essentially whoredom. Eve is anything but a whore.

"Nor is she the proverbial wet-lipped starlet who makes

27

all the Gala Openings wearing two shoelaces over her tits and a glaze on her eyes. Some cheap-jack agent has told her that'll do it for her. It won't, it never has. Jayne Mansfield's neck-to-navel probably made more magazine covers than J. Kennedy Onassis *plus* Audrey Hepburn, drew mobs at supermarket openings and roller derbies — and emptied theatres. Oh, of course screwing your way into a bit part or screen test can be so often more persuasive than reading for them — but I can think of no instance in which a truly important role, a demanding and significant one, has been 'cast on a couch,' to coin a cliché. Anyway, none of this has to do with Eve. This has to do with commerce, not ambition.

"Eve is essentially — in the theatre, *Harpers Bazaar*, *Vogue*, I.B.M., or wherever — the girl unceasingly, relentlessly on the make. Not necessarily for men; as a matter of fact, only rarely. A particular man, perhaps, or series of men — or women — may be the means to an important end, but almost never the ultimate goal. That goal — toward which Eve is fanatically and forever at full charge — is no less than all of whatever there is to be had.

("I know I seem to be indicating that the Eve *drang* is exclusively feminine; it's not, of course. It is a deeply rooted obsessive male/female need, an insatiably greedy one, to acquire more and more and more — but *not* necessarily money or possessions; indeed, very rarely tangibles of any kind. And its manifestations appear no more frequently in one sex than the other. Eve has to do, after all, with much of what also made Sammy run.)

"That insatiable need and greed. You will remember that they become even more intolerable to Eve, in the end, than they have been to us all along. Because she is confronted in the end — as all Eves must be, and are — by an acute aware-

28

ness that, in fact, ever since the beginning, she has been servicing a bottomless pit. A void. Her ego? That Self, without which nobody is anybody? The Eves — male and/or female — have none. Just an inner emptiness they can never fill — but must continue to feed, merely to exist. Such, exactly, was the human condition of our heroine when we first came upon her in my film.

"Gertrude Slescynski (the name and person Eve had discarded) had rendered herself literally nonexistent. Not one facet of Gertrude's previous life or personality did she consider worthy of inclusion in the Eve Harrington she fabricated for the wooing of Margo and the others. Gertrude/Eve was of course unaware, consciously, that she had no more depth of identity than a cartoon. How could she have been aware? When her existence up to that point had undoubtedly been a montage of hundreds of such fabrications?

"Actually, I clobbered Eve with self-knowledge long before her co-predators are forced to face it, as a rule. Usually it hits them only after the pickings have grown thin. When they're getting on. When the dissembling has come to require more effort, the lying become less intuitive and the lies less valid. When the equipment's grown old or outmoded — or they've just gone as far as they're going to go. From that point on they sulk a lot, drink a lot, scrounge for small favors — but it's downhill to nothing, and they know it. You gather I don't like Eve? You're right. I've been there. I've seen what they can do to living people, the scars they can leave. The most virulent Eve I've ever known was the production head of a major studio.

"Nobody (I'm back to my film, now) could have 'told' Eve Harrington what she was. Or wasn't, if you will. Honest insight into one's self is rarely acceptable from external sources;

there are simply too many compensating equivocations available to an even minimally resourceful neurotic. No, it has to come up from within one — explode, more often than not — and has to be an experience of self-confrontation that cannot be evaded or transformed into a more tolerable substitute. That's why it was only under the relentless pressure of Addison's devastation of her masquerade — only after he had thoroughly sealed off every possible escape route — that I felt justified, at the very peak of her hysteria and terror, in having Eve give voice to her first acknowledgment of the emptiness she was and had always been: 'I had to say something, *be somebody!*'

"I'm sure you understand by now — God knows I've gone on long enough about it — that it was Gertrude Slescynski who blubbered those words up at Addison, not Eve. Gertrude, who had been nothing, justifying her creating of Eve — who would be everything. And now that the breakthrough had happened — it could not unhappen. Eve would never be altogether Eve again. And as her self-awareness increased, so the others being 'on' to her mattered less.

"I made that clear, I think. At the end, after the award ceremony, for instance. Eve's listlessness, almost a numbness, one type of the 'post-award depression' I spoke about earlier (a sort of reverse alchemy: the gold, as you hold it, turns into shit). Her vague searching for drink, her sulky unwillingness to go to the party in her honor. Addison, completely aware, remonstrates patiently: 'Max has gone to a great deal of trouble, it's going to be an elaborate party, and it's for you.' Eve holds up, and refers to, the Award: 'No, it's not. It's for this.' Addison couldn't agree more: 'It's the same thing, isn't it?' 'Exactly,' says Eve.

"Even more pertinent to my point, I think, was to make

it evident that Margo now knew all about Eve. And that Eve knew she knew. Witness Margo's 'congratulatory' remark to her upon the same occasion: ' . . . nice speech, Eve. But I wouldn't worry too much about your heart. You can always put that Award where your heart ought to be.' That about sums up Eve, I think."

All About Eve has usually been regarded only as a satire preoccupied with the New York theatre. Actually, Mankiewicz places it within a series of consecutive films (*Letter To Three Wives*, 1949; *House of Strangers*, 1949; *People Will Talk*, 1951; *No Way Out*, 1950; *Five Fingers*, 1952) in which he attempted "a continuing comment on the manners-and-mores of our contemporary society in general, and the male–female interrelationship in particular." In fact, as he discusses his characters, it becomes clear that this latter aspect was as important to Mankiewicz as was giving the low-down on the dog-eat-dog world of Broadway. Though these relationships may be somewhat atypical because they are set against the extraordinary background of the theatre, they still have wider application. Margo's identity problems are not only to be found in the theatre and, as Mankiewicz has said, there are Eves in all professions of life. Similarly, while the emotional problems of the third major female character, Karen Richards, are also spotlighted by her involvement with the theatre, they are the most universal, for her sole career is that of wife.

Karen is another great variant upon her counterpart in the Orr story. In the original, she is an actress, not quite first-rate (or so it is implied), and she has a tongue as cheap and acid-tipped as Clare Boothe's characters in *The Women*. Mankiewicz, however, had a much different concept he wanted to explore with this character, set off from the others by her nonprofessional standing:

"Of all the females that inhabit the society of theatre-folk, the one for whom I have always felt the greatest compassion is she for whom, in that society, only one role is available: that of 'wife to————.' As in the *dramatis personae* of Elizabethan plays, her billing (i.e., tribal status) is far down the list. With luck, she will be identified as a specific 'wife to ————.' (As in 'Calpurnia, wife to Caesar'; 'Margaret, wife to Mayer'; 'Virginia, wife to Zanuck'; 'Legion, wife to Rooney,' and so on). More often than not, she is lumped anonymously among: 'Courtiers, Lords and Ladies in attendance, and gentlewomen-in-waiting.'

"They're in waiting, all right, these 'wives to ————.' Day and night, increasingly as time goes on — waiting. For the axe, the heave-ho, the marital pink slip. For that increasingly foreseeable tumbrel trip to the divorce court. (For some reason I've never asked about, movie people usually divorce themselves in Santa Monica, California, a community otherwise notable only for a little-known statue of Myrna Loy at the foot of Wilshire Boulevard — and a teeming ghetto of rather elegant homosexuals, cashiered to the Pacific from their origins elsewhere within our Great Silent Morality.)

"Anyway, before that court she will produce evidence of irreconcilable incompatibility; the property settlement having already been negotiated by professionals trained in the *quid pro quo* of how-much-money for how-much-misery. The interlocutory decree of divorce will be handed down, a ritual every bit as impressive as being slipped a baggage check. She will then return to a house of which she may or may not

32

have been granted custody — stripped of a marriage which had totally absorbed anywhere from ten to forty years of her adult existence. An ex- 'wife to ———.' Very much alone.

"As an alien among the native citizenry of theatre-folk, resident only by virtue of marriage to one of them, her 'visa' remains valid for only the duration of that relationship. Once it's over, she becomes a foreign body and quick removal is indicated. Sometimes they won't accept that premise, these ex- 'wives to ———.' They've made 'friends of their own' among the theatre-folk, they insist, sharing interests other than the last play, the present film, the future commitments to stage or studio or TV. They're wrong, they haven't. There are no other interests, in fact, among theatre-folk.

"The activities generated by these 'wives to ———,' which, hopefully, will sustain for them the illusion that they have found 'lives of their own' — or that they contribute importantly to the careers and lives of their mates — may include political activism, community affairs, and the pursuit of self-improvement (Let's hear it for those extension courses at U.C.L.A., Columbia, and The New School). No matter. These and other efforts, however assiduously pursued, are invariably regarded by theatre-folk to be nothing more than the hobbies and diversions to which the nonprofessional must turn to pass time. Like masturbation and billing, of real concern only to those immediately involved.

"To be sure, if her body has retained sufficient attraction — and sometimes even if it hasn't, even if she just makes it available — the most recent ex- 'wife to ———' may attract some early action in bed. For one thing, among theatre-folk, there's that corps of strange studs — their motivations have always fascinated me — who specialize in servicing, sexually, the newly widowed and newly divorced female. As quickly as possible after the fact of the funeral or divorce decree.

33

I imagine it's a sort of vicarious necrophilia; probably the one they're really 'screwing' is the dead, or departed, husband. Certainly not, I think, the confused and despairing woman who has quite naturally overreacted to an indication of affection.

"The studs move on, though, as swiftly as they moved in. The kids, if they're grown up — and they might well be — extend the proper assurances, go through the proper motions, and then go about living their own lives. Quite rightly. What next, then? For this woman, no longer young by the standards of a society that sets a stringent early limit upon the female right to youth and its benefits — now cut adrift at age anywhere from thirty-five to fifty-five — suddenly a stranger and afraid in a world she never made and thank you, Mr. Housman . . . ?

"About Karen. When I wrote Addison DeWitt's capsulized summary of her as: '. . . the wife of a playwright, therefore of the Theatre by marriage. Nothing in her background or breeding should have brought her any closer to the stage than row E, Center.' — actually, I was stacking the circumstances in her favor. Those who are of the Theatre only by marriage, or other emotional attachment to one of its native citizenry, usually have neither the intellectual capacity nor the emotional stability of a Karen. Yet she, too, was a foreigner, an émigrée from what a producer's wife once described to me as 'private people.' And in common with all other 'wives to —————' among the theatre-folk, Karen, too, faced an ultimate probable expendability.

("I don't know why I feel I must periodically point out that these theatre-folk types exist in both genders. Of course there are 'husbands to —————,' as well. But, as always, the male is luckier and has many more disguises available for camouflaging his inferior status. And usually, among

34

theatre-folk, the Wife of Importance will actually connive at the masquerade of her schmuck husband; witness the prevalence of 'general managers,' 'executive and/or associate producers,' 'creative consultants,' and other smoke-ring designations for the husbands of theatrical Wives of Importance. He can carry her make-up kit right on the stage and retain his *machismo*. The 'wife to ———' rarely dares so much as a visit to the theatre-folk at their work. Not if she has even an instinct for survival, she doesn't.)

"But when had this female of the 'private people' been essential to the male of the theatre-folk who married her? At what point had she been so desperately needed — under what circumstance was functioning without her so impossible for him — that marriage became a necessity? When they were both very young. When she needed him — and he needed his needs. When they spoke love, which is a very imprecise language — and not at all a specific emotion. Just about everything that anybody has ever demanded of anybody else — has been called love. But that's a different cassette.

"She wasn't 'wife to ———' back then. No, sir. Back then she was — right out of the catalogue — wife. Meaning also: mother; cook/laundress; childbearer; accountant; partner and professional consultant; whipping post (with understanding: 'an Artist has to take it out on somebody,' right?) for his frustrations and failures; sexually, whenever and whatever he wanted (her own pleasure relatively unimportant: 'a Man needs relief,' right?) for his tensions and insecurities. And he? What was he, where was he? A couple of generations ago, out in his junkyard, maybe. Or looking up from cutting gloves and shirts — perhaps from collecting fares on a trolley car — to stare at that movie nickelodeon on the corner. To dream of owning a factory to supply it with 'product.'

"Or — in a later generation — on another, more creative

level. Auditioning, 'making the rounds,' more auditioning, blowing the rent money for classes in acting and/or directing. Those 'classes.' Usually conducted by actors and/or directors whose qualifications to teach acting and/or directing seemingly go unchallenged except by those who have successfully acted and directed. *Or* — that tiresome but nonetheless valid cliché — asleep by day and up all night, at the kitchen table, typing at the play or the book — posting the fat envelopes, haunting the mailbox for skinny replies. But always, in all these instances, *her* mission, her reason for *being*: to sustain hope for them both, to make do with what there was, and, above all, to keep fixed *his* position as the shining center of the universe.

"Those, although she couldn't know it at the time, were the best years she would ever know. Especially when they were ultimately culminated by that Moment, Day or Night of Triumph. (We speak, after all, of the Successful. The Failures, that vast majority — they just went on with their limited lives and long marriages of mutual recrimination.)

"So witness our heroines: a generation or so ago, the junk dealer's/glover's/trolley conductor's wife on her first ride to the West. That drawing room aboard the Twentieth-Century Limited, the layover at the Blackstone in Chicago with its marble bathtubs and cattle-baron elegance, and then the Santa Fe Chief for three nights and two days — luxuriating by day, only half-listening to his endless planning with his new partners — movie retailers all — at long last on their way to build factories in California for the manufacture of 'product.' And at night, after a dinner she hadn't had to cook, being humped in a bouncing berth she hadn't had to make up, enjoying it even, permitting herself the hope that, at long last, her life would include joy.

36

"And now a quick cut to that later, other generation. (We used to utilize dissolves for a time lapse that long, quite rightly — anywhere from eight to twenty feet. European film labs made lousy dissolves then, so bad they couldn't be used, and European directors fumed and fussed but were forced to make do with the straight cut. Then discovered, to their utter amazement, that early U.S. cinéastes were hailing them for having developed a new editing technique. But now that the film labs abroad are by far the best in the world . . . but that, too, is a different cassette.)

"However we get there, let's make the setting obvious and to the point. It's that Night of Triumph at — you guessed it — Sardi's. The critic of *The New York Times* has just been observed still dancing on Forty-fourth Street. The TV reviewers, unanimous raves, have been permitted to usurp as much as fourteen seconds of the weather outlook for Northern Greenland, thus extending to almost two full minutes their thoughtful appraisals of a work representing possibly two years of the creative lives of many artists. But 'they've made it.' The playwright-husband is now 'a new and vigorous talent — a witty and trenchant observer of the current scene.' The director-husband is no longer 'professional, capable and sound' — tonight 'he created that interplay of movement and mood and dramatic impact that make for magic in the theatre.' And the actor-husband — this night 'he came gloriously into his own, master now of his techniques, drawing upon a now richly matured and bountiful talent.'

"As for their young wives — awash with champagne and blissful tears — there never was, never would be, another Night such as this. They were being rewarded with the most that any vicarious participation in glory ever provides: a happy conviction that their years of self-denial, of drudgery and devotion, had made a very real contribution to this Great Moment. As, indeed, they had. There might, during that Night of Triumph, even be public acknowledgment of that contribution: 'her night as much as mine...' 'her faith in me, the times I was ready to just quit . . .' all to be heard from the lips of Don Ameche and Ty Power on the Late Show, but none the less valid. And later that Night, at home alone in ecstatic privacy, he might even whisper it just to her: 'We've made it, you and I. We've made it.'

"But *they* haven't, of course. Not among the theatre-folk. *He* has. Remember those services she'd performed as wife — so desperately needed by the Artist, so essential to his functioning at all? 'Mother'? The Mass Audience will replace her, there. They'll give suck to him, spoil, scold, cuddle, and reject him in a variety of ways beyond her power even to imagine. Cooks and house-cleaners will be hired now, of course, and come and go as they do, and her domestic duties will become that of personnel manager for backward delinquents.

"Childbearer? Oh, she'll want children rather soon if she doesn't already have some. If for no other reason than as a reassurance, to herself, of her physical presence — as a sort of sea anchor to control her drift. Then she'll discover that, among theatre-folk, children become almost always the sole responsibility of the non-performing parent; there is almost always too large an area of competition between the child and the performing parent.

"What else? Partner — wailing wall — even whipping post? Forget it. What with producers, packagers, lawyers, agents, business managers, publicity men, secretaries — his professional life and income will become so compartmen-

38

talized and overstructured that he, himself, will rarely know what they are. Annually, she will sign a joint income-tax return where designated. At specific intervals, regular deposits will be made in what is called her 'household account.' She as far as her contribution to her husband's life is concerned, will become one of the smaller moving parts in a mechanism.

"Sex? No need to go into that, why belabor the obvious. It's not surprising, really, the readiness with which the 'wife to ———' adjusts to sexual infidelity by her spouse. After all, he does come home; her visa does remain valid.

"What she does dread, lives in terror of, is — serious emotional involvement on his part. It could happen any day. Her man doesn't leave of a morning, after all, for a corporate structure in which he merely fills a niche. No, this husband goes off to a fun fair where he's the brass ring on the merry-go-round; a nonstop Miss Universe contest and the one he smiles on goes into orbit. He's fair game every minute he's away from home. At the studio, the audition, the rehearsal — it can happen while waiting for a traffic light to change. That involvement. An Eve in the car alongside. Meanwhile, back at home, the 'wife to ———' can do nothing but wait. And play out her role, that of being 'in-waiting.' For as many years as she lasts.

"You know, I've written about a lot of women — most of the time not as truthfully or perceptively as I would have liked to, for various reasons — and I've speculated about hundreds. They're my favorite humans. Pondering men, by comparison, is staring at alphabet blocks. And I can't think of, I couldn't dream up, a human being more truly helpless than the 'wife to ———,' at this point, among the theatre-folk.

"She is completely helpless. Without weapons. Her physi-

39

cal attractions are faded; at their best, they were no match for those, the best in the world, that now beguile her husband relentlessly. His former dependence upon her has been fragmented and distributed among those whose profession it is to keep him dependent. He no longer needs her. Not at all. Nor has she allies; after all, she can do nothing for anyone. Not even herself. Except hope for him to come home — and prepare for the time when he doesn't. She is a civilian casualty, unwept and unsung, among the theatre folk.

"Yes, I liked Karen more than any of the others. She was more aware — less ignorant, rather — of what the theatre, and she in it, was all about. So witness her musing — when she recalls the night Lloyd left her to go to Eve: 'It seemed to me I had known always that it would happen — and here it was. I felt helpless, that helplessness you feel when you have no talent to offer — outside of loving your husband. How could I compete? Everything Lloyd loved about me, he had gotten used to long ago . . .' "

In conception, Karen is the film's most original character. Mankiewicz' admiration for her is evidenced by the writing of the part; she is the most intelligent, dignified, and warm person in the story. "I endowed Karen with intelligence and taste," Mankiewicz recalls, "because to the extent that they possess those virtues, the disquietudes and frustrations of women become ever more complex — and fascinating. And because the well-bred and well-spoken have become a dwindling minority in a society in which, too often, witless rudeness passes as a badge of merit."

Just as in many other Mankiewicz films, the female characters are more vividly drawn than the men in *All About Eve*. When I asked him if it were fair to say that as a writer, he was more attracted to women and their problems, he answered:

"Fair? I'm well-nigh besotted by them. Writing about men is so damned . . . limited. They're made up, for the most part, of large, predictable, conforming elements. Men react as they're taught to react, in what they've been taught is a 'manly' way. Women are, by comparison, as if assembled by the wind. They're made up of — and react to — tiny impulses. Inflections. Colors. Sounds. They hear things men cannot. And, further, react to stimuli men either can't feel or must reject as 'unmanly.' 'Unmanly.' Whatever the hell that means. Of a kind with 'virtuous,' I suppose. Part of the dogma set down by a manly and virtuous society to which our evolving genders must adhere. A surprisingly large proportion of females do not. A shockingly large proportion of males do. And you'll find that the rules of 'manliness' restrict the writer about men almost as much as they do the male who submits to them.

"It would be fascinating to do a film about a man in rebellion against 'manliness.' (Not necessarily a homosexual. There's another of our society's rigidities: you're either 'manly' or queer. The simplistic Agnewistic black-or-white ploy — if you're not with us, you're against us — America and 'manliness' — love 'em or leave 'em. Homosexuals — male and female — are constituents of a thoroughly viable third sex. Within it, the chances of success or failure in personal interrelationships need be neither more nor less than within any other. *If*, that is, our 'virtuous' and 'manly' society drops its vendetta against them.) Anyway . . . the film about the man in revolt against 'manliness': I'd like to tell it by suggestion, by nuance and mood, by utilizing all of the subjective techniques and material you're supposed to eschew in portraying the male on stage or screen. Why the hell, for

41

instance, shouldn't a man burst into tears? Or lose badly? Or be indecisive — or be irrationally afraid of the unknown or unseen — or smell good — or want peace?

"No, the 'man's role,' as presently in vogue, doesn't interest me very much as writer and/or director. He is invariably expected to pit himself physically against his adversary: to me, the least imaginative and interesting form of confrontation. His goals are usually restricted to, variously, conquering or amassing things. A fortune of money, an enemy country, a chain of factories, a series of broads — one or more loathsome children who, quite understandably, find him equally loathsome — in short, acquisitions. His conflicts, overt and incomplex all, are resolved by physical action, usually violent.

"Far-fetched generalization? Not all that much. Examine the recent spate of so-called 'youth-oriented,' 'anti-establishment' films. When, ever, were the creative spokesmen for a generation granted such an extensive platform from which to expound and clarify the substance of its objectives? Name those films — count them on your thumbs — which reflected the slightest vestige of inner conflict, the emotional strains and stresses of cerebral decision, cerebration of any kind, for that matter. Name those in which the opposing forces were not 'stacked' with childish simplicity on a par with that which used to put black hats on Noah Beery and his nasty rustlers — and white hats on Tom Mix and his true-blue cowboys. *Strawberry Statement, Getting Straight, Zabriskie Point,* countless other revolutionary potboilers before and since. (And I do mean 'pot.') What struck me was how far back they reached — to the very beginnings of filmmaking — to resolve the presumably complex problems they posed. In the last reel, the White Hats simply kick the shit out of the Black Hats. And everybody goes home happy. Just like the good old days.

"I'm quite aware that what we used to call 'heading 'em off at the pass' is now known as 'confrontation' or, even less to the point, 'happening.' But even the reality 'happenings' — and certainly the films about them — seem to have no more intellectual implication, and little more pertinence, than the old-time dynamite blast in the mine shaft. Blowing up a college is not an answer to educational inequities or idiocies. It doesn't solve the problem; it merely blows it up. Pissing on a church is hardly a valid comment on the medieval restrictiveness of organized religions; it's a cheap and infantile substitute for thought. If the writer and/or director is incapable of the latter, he must not be permitted to piss away our time and attention on the former. Confine him to a projection room, make him run the films of Federico Fellini over and over and over — and study his craft."

Mankiewicz cited this "preoccupation with externals" as one of the reasons he didn't think he would be writing films for a while:

"Besides which, women are rarely represented on the screen these days, except as tits. Do you want to make a million dollars? Discover the biggest Star of all time? Be the first to come up with a beautiful girl with square tits. It seems to me that's what they must be searching for. Why else should the female mammary gland have replaced the ringing telephone as the movies' most photographed insert?"

All About Eve does, however, contain one dynamically drawn male character, Addison DeWitt, the acerbic critic who gives Eve her comeuppance. According to Mankiewicz:

43

"Addison's essential motivations and instincts are those of a collector. True, an acceptable male objective, the acquisition of possessions. But the items he collects are the most subjective imaginable: the secret fears, the private peccadillos of other people. His ultimate goal, of course, is dominance over them — and their work. As a critic-commentator among the theatre folk, as a noncontributive bystander — it's as if all of their lives were somehow a continuing auction, and he empowered always to bid highest. Note, please, that his superiority to his antagonists is cerebral; he doesn't blow them up. And note also that Addison DeWitt, as an inhabitant of the Theatre, is a greatly exaggerated character. His component parts exist — and have existed — in reality. But not the sum total of them. Not nearly."

(The scene between Addison and Eve in the New Haven hotel room is sex-as-politics — a startlingly modern idea for a film made in 1950. One in which 'killer' meets 'killer' — Eve 'steps up in class' — and Addison proves himself, as he had warned Eve, 'champion.')

"To a certain extent, in some of his externals — his 'asides,' as it were — Addison is me," Mankiewicz continued. "His comments on the nature of the actor, for instance, and also those on the pontifications of the elder statesmen of stage and screen." This rather eyebrow-raising admission was mitigated as he continued. "There's always a character — sometimes more than one — that's me in the films I've written. Why should that surprise you? I'm a film-heretic — anathema to those who find it so much easier to point a camera than direct an actor. I'm known to be committed to the heresy that the word can be at least as contributive to the non-epic film as the lens. I am also known to prefer actors trained in speaking to those who just grunt through hair. My films talk

44

a lot — hell, *I* talk a lot; have you any cassettes left? At best, I suppose, hopefully I've been, at times, a witty and perhaps trenchant commentator on the manners and mores of our society. At worst, a describer, let's say, of various aspects of the human condition and the social background against which it endures. At the very worst — a bore. But, then, simply because my talents may not live up to my standards is certainly no reason to abandon those standards."

It has generally been assumed that Addison was based on George Jean Nathan, the acidulous theatre critic whose reviews between 1920 and 1950 were considered by many to have been more outrageous than accurate. There are certain similarities between Nathan and DeWitt: the acerbic tongue, the fastidiousness of dress, and the dramatic cigarette holder. Also, some aspects of the relationship between Eve and Addison suggest a parallel to the friendship between Nathan and his various protégées, as, for example, Julie Haydon.* When I asked Mankiewicz to confirm this supposition, he replied, "In his mannerisms and posturings, I suppose Addison reflects some of those of George Nathan — but not to the exclusion of many others on the periphery of the creative community." But certainly, I pointed out, Addison's anti-Hollywood bias was drawn directly from Nathan's vitriolic stance on America's film-making capital. Mankiewicz concurred only in part:

"That 'vitriolic stance' of Nathan's, as you put it, was probably, to a large extent, as much of a façade as the 'Holly-

---

* Nathan first met Julie Haydon when she was making the Hecht-MacArthur film, *The Scoundrel* (1935). He was instrumental in getting her her first important lead on Broadway, *Shadow and Substance* (1938). Miss Haydon's most famous role was as Laura in the original production of *The Glass Menagerie* (1945).

wood' against which it was directed. You must bear in mind that even critics — especially critics — have their personality-aliases. Today more than ever, I would say, now that criticism is quite obviously on its way to becoming just one more of the performing arts. Actually, I look to the emergence of a new form of criticism — one which will render impersonal, unimpeachable critiques of the performances of our contemporary critics and their pseudocritical shenanigans.

"Critics have acquired all of the managerial trappings of performers, you know; their tradition is no longer so much that of William Winter* as William Morris. Their writings, even their opinions, are too often obviously intended either to establish or enhance their individual 'box-office draw' as 'personalities' — with a dismayingly canny and commercial eye on the public marketplace. (Ah, those juicy fees for speaking tours amongst the community-culture circuits. So rewarding to both ego and pocketbook, especially if immediately preceded by a well-publicized, mercilessly witty savaging of a major new work by some — preferably native — author, playwright, or film maker. Or, increasingly popular these days, the mercilessly witty savaging of another critic. Have you noticed how, more and more, they seem to be writing for, about, and against, one another? Today's proverbial Gentle Reader, in search of objective and qualified opinion about a new play, film, or book, more often than not winds up being

---

* William Winter (1836–1917). Dramatic critic of the New York *Tribune* from 1865 until he retired in 1909. Highly esteemed by the world of the theatre, considered the dean of dramatic criticism in America. In 1916 a unique memorial was tendered him, signed not only by most of the leading contemporary actors, actresses, and playwrights but also by President Woodrow Wilson, Theodore Roosevelt, and William H. Taft among other prominent public figures.

46

told more than he wants to know, really, about the deficiencies of another critic.)

"You know, I've never been quite sure of what the qualifications are for, say, a film critic. Surely not just the experience of having looked at, and digested, thousands of movies. By that criterion, half my class at college would have qualified. But I can stipulate one essential prerequisite for the present-day critic who would attain that ultimate of critical attainments — the power to affect the popular acceptance or rejection of a creative effort. He or she had damn well better be photogenic and without lisp or stutter. Therein — to the degree to which he possesses equipment hitherto essential only to the performer — may well lie his ultimate critical status. His verdict either accepted as unquestioningly as is the laxative commercial which follows it, by millions of television viewers — or relegated to the negligibly few, haphazardly interested readers of *Women's Wear Daily, The New Leader,* and other consumer guides.

"Back to George Nathan and his fellow 'Hollywood' baiters of the thirties and forties. (After the early fifties — after Television folk inundated the area — using 'Hollywood' as an epithet became a critical cop-out, really. Some critics still do, of course. When they can't, or won't bother to, analyze their dislike for a film or its creators. Calling something 'Hollywood' today is just a cheap shot. Whipping a horse that's not only dead but disintegrated.) But back then, in what has now come to be known as 'The Golden Age' for reasons which escape me, Nathan and many other professional denigrators of 'Hollywood' spent more time out there than you might think.

"Harold Ross, for one. Founder, editor, and czar of *The New Yorker.* Harold was famous for the edict that he cared

47

not who his film critic was, as long as he hated movies. I have always been of the opinion that one of the most contributive elements to Harold's intense dislike for Hollywood was the fact that so many of his friends, over the years, deserted New York — and *The New Yorker* — to go out there. He was a gregarious man (with a chosen few), and resented the great inconvenience of having to travel three thousand miles to visit with the wit and talent he had been accustomed to find in an adjoining office — or certainly no further away than the Algonquin. But Hollywood was where they were — and Harold came out. Often. As a matter of fact, Harold Ross was chiefly responsible for one of the few bastions of good taste ever to endure in Southern California: Chasen's Restaurant.

"Ross had known Dave Chasen ever since Dave had been Joe Cook's top banana in Vaudeville and on Broadway. (Chasen and Joe Cook, along with Ted Healy, Frank Tinney, Bobby Clark, Leon Errol, and Frank Fay — just for starters — were some of what made people laugh before *The Beverly Hillbillies*.) Chasen worked with a red wig and a blacked-out tooth, and came out with Joe Cook to do a film for Columbia. Frank Capra directed. It was called *Rain or Shine*, I believe, and Joe Cook never made another film as far as I know. Financially, he had no problems; he'd saved a lot of money during the fat years on Broadway. But Dave Chasen had nothing to fall back on but the red wig and the blacked-out tooth — *and* a talent for making the best chili and barbecued spareribs this side of anywhere — *and* many good friends that ranged, socially, intellectually, and financially from Ross and Nunnally Johnson to Jock Whitney. So, with Harold Ross as godfather and chief backer, Dave Chasen opened what was, to begin with, no more than a glorified chili, spareribs, and hamburger joint, in the mid-1930's, exactly where it is today — ever an oasis for the unassimilated Eastern palate exiled to the land of The Prime Rib.

"The activities of George Jean Nathan, and others of his ilk, were less gastronomical. George enjoyed, shall we say, the company of extremely beautiful young women with extremely limited mentalities — who would listen. He was not a lone prospector, believe me. For the intellectual on the prowl, Hollywood, at the time, was a veritable Klondike. The place was chock-a-block with ravishing young females, many of international renown, hungry to be appreciated for qualities they had not. Like the nothing-but-rich who want to be loved for anything but their money, these babes would genuflect before anyone qualified to endorse their claim to even the faintest glimmer of cerebral capacity. The awesome physical attributes of the young Adonises who swarmed about these beauties like suntanned ants, attracted them not at all. If anything, their steel-muscled, flat-bellied male counterparts were irritants: they tended to emphasize the anatomical hollows and protuberances upon which their own fame rested. Barely capable of spelling out the screenplays they were enacting, they wanted so much to be sought after as more than just one cute ass or two sun-kissed tits — oh, if only they hadn't dropped out of high school and if only they could remember whether it was George Eliot or George Sand who was really a woman . . .

"The cultivation of these minuscule mentalities was a game that George Nathan and many other marauding *litterateurs* delighted in playing during their occasional sojournings out there. Almost the most successful sexual ploy in Hollywood during the thirties and forties (far more productive than the fox cape or diamond anklet) was, quite simply, a list of books which the visiting — or resident — intellectual would draw up for the edification and education of the

49

culture-hungry screen beauty. (For some reason, *Zuleika Dobson* — 'Max must have had you in mind when he wrote it . . .' — was on all the lists. Another favorite was the collected verse of Edna St. Vincent Millay, which the lip-reading cuties would underscore heavily, usually with eyebrow pencils, as giving precise voice to their own troubled hearts.) Whether or not they actually read the books, they bought all of them; merely acquiring the complete list provided for them the equivalent of an intellectual mink coat they could wear proudly and publicly. (What greater legacy, after all, could Scott Fitzgerald have left to Sheilah Graham than her delusion of literacy?)

"At any rate, whatever the relationship between illiterate Beauty and lettered Beast it was merely one of the relatively undamaging, and for the most part enjoyable, fringe benefits to be garnered on the outskirts of the theatre-folk corral out there. I certainly didn't intend to equate the Addison–Eve alliance — an unholy one, of mutual mistrust and manipulation — with any of those I've been nattering about. Eve was no starry-eyed babe in search of a mind to improve. Nor is there, as I've already pointed out, any substantial basis for a serious identification of Addison DeWitt with George Jean Nathan.

"I think it was probably Addison's unashamed and overt theatricality that attracted you so much to him as a character. It was intended to. Whenever your villain becomes a bore, whatever you're writing — play, film, whatever — wrap it up, abandon ship. Conversely, first-rate villains very often, by the mere reflection of the infinitely greater attractiveness and scope that villainy has over virtue, will endow the most numbing of dullard heroes and heroines with an appeal they couldn't possibly attain on their own. From Mephistopheles to Rupert of Hentzau. It's my guess Will Shakespeare found

Iago a breeze to write compared to Othello; and that he sweated more over Brutus than Cassius. No further resemblance intended, or even hinted at, of course.

"I hurry to throw that in because once, in defense of my position that the offstage or offscreen moral and/or political propensities of creative talents should not be applicable to a judgment of their work, I used Michelangelo as an example. I said that I doubted very much whether anyone gazing for the first time at the ceiling of the Sistine Chapel had ever been repelled by knowing that its creator had been a pederast. Nor, as far as I knew, had it been of concern to Pope Julius II who must have been aware of Signor Buonarroti's sexual nuances but who nevertheless hired him to do the job. My remarks were passed on (second-handedly, by his own admission) to Dwight Macdonald, a whilom critic whose judgments, while oozing papal infallibility, rarely stooped to clemency. Mr. Macdonald promptly handed down the pronouncement (from the pages of whatever magazine then served as his pulpit), in evaluating my involvement with the most absurdly traumatic experience of my professional life, that I had quite seriously compared myself to Michelangelo! So — I must be forgiven a certain amount of apprehension when, in the course of being interviewed or otherwise saying what might be repeated or printed, I allude, while making a point, to artists and works of a quality of genius which is, as yet, many light-years away from the furthest horizons of film-making."

I indicated to Mankiewicz that I had found the remaining male characters in *Eve* sketchily drawn. It has been conjectured that Bill Sampson, the young director with whom Margo was in love, was based in part upon the young Elia

Kazan. He and Mankiewicz have long been good friends; they share similar views about many aspects of both the theatre and film-making. For example, Sampson's no-non-sense attitude towards both the theatre and working in it (as illustrated in his sounding-off to Eve in Margo's dressing room) is, Mankiewicz admitted:

"Not unlike Gadg's own non-horseshit approach to his profession. In his case, it sets free his great talent. However, too many of our steadily employed colleagues have unhappily too little talent to set free. Accordingly, they keep on apply-ing layer after layer of 'theatuh' bushwah — like house paint. It seems to work, horseshit being a basic commodity in both 'theatuh' and 'cinemah.' It abounds throughout the entire spectrum of American theatrical activity; from our most pretentious, oversubsidized and calamitous attempt at reper-tory (here in New York City) — up or down to the innu-merable 'Drama Schools' on the university level, where the instillation of 'theatuh' is prescribed by curriculum and the damage begun."

I continued to argue the point that in my opinion Bill wasn't really fleshed out enough to become an interesting character. That, in fact, I found him rather bothersome. After that initial characteristic aria to Eve, he's defined almost entirely by his soothing effect on Margo's tirades, and his endless good sense and babying eventually become patroniz-ing. Similarly, it seemed to me that Lloyd Richards had very little personality or existence beyond what was demanded from his reaction to the other characters and the action. Actually his plays, which, it is indicated, derive from the Tennessee Williams school of Southern depravity, struck me as better defined than he was. Mankiewicz disagreed with my criticisms of both Bill and Lloyd:

"Perhaps you found Bill not 'interesting' and Lloyd wanting in 'personality' because of the absence of overt theatricality in their private and professional behavior. (Even so, not a total absence: Lloyd does have his screaming playwright–actress confrontation with Margo, ending with his 'It's about time the piano realizes it has not written the concerto!' And Bill, in a temperament tantrum, does walk out on the rehearsal of Lloyd's new play.) On the whole, they're what I intended them to be: two talented craftsmen, one a director and one a writer, who have worked hard and long and responsibly at their craft within a theatre which they love — and within which they earn their livelihoods.

"Lloyd relates the production of his plays to his personal financial concerns, as well he might. As a playwright, he is not, as he points out, 'an oil well operator.' Therefore he is not preferentially treated by a society which refuses to concede that a human talent is either as important, or as subject to depletion, as a geological deposit. He is well aware of the contrasting demands of the make-believe world in which he practices his craft — and the very real one he encounters as he steps out of the stage door. He lives expensively. A snazzy duplex in town; also a country home. He and Karen dress well, eat well, probably travel and entertain a lot.

("By the way, your analogy to Tennessee Williams — except for the fact that Tennessee was, at the time I wrote *All About Eve*, both headmaster and head-of-the-class of an entire school of writers about Southern sexual proclivities — is not otherwise even remotely applicable. If you must have a frame of reference for Lloyd, I could suggest many candidates: Phil Barry, Bob Sherwood, Moss Hart, Sam Behrman, et al. — all eminently talented, highly successful and partial to the good life.)

"When playwriting is your only profession, your only source not just of gratification but also food and shelter and covering for your nakedness — whether in the theatre, film or, the Saints preserve us, television — you learn very quickly that the successful craftsman must be responsive to more than just capturing, on one hundred and twenty pages more or less, the freewheeling fancies of his Muse. He must be aware of, and understand, and face the workaday practicalities of making his living in the theatre, film or, the Saints preserve us, television.

"Art? Yes, I have studiously avoided using the word. If it has slipped out, it's been by inadvertence, believe me. Art — with a big A, to set it apart from its general connotation of highly developed skill — is a designation I'm extremely chary about using. Another one is: Genius with a big G. We live in a time of instant coffee, soup, cake mix, copulation — also instant Genius. They carry the label but neither the content nor the quality of the original, more slowly arrived at, product. They're ersatz. Our language has the largest goddamn vocabulary in the Western world, and the lack of selectivity with which we use it appalls me.

"Year in and year out our creative talents turn out a few first-rate books, plays, and films which reflect, at most, superb craftsmanship — and of which too many are frivolously, even casually, hailed as Works of Art. (I once witnessed, on what I believe is called Educational Television, the resident *cinéaste* quite seriously extolling the texture of a wall, in front of which Monica Vitti — I think — was posing in an — I think — Antonioni film, as being subtly contributive to the aesthetic purpose of the Master. Now, I had personally utilized that same wall — or its exact duplicate — in at least two of my own movies. The plaster shop at Cinécittà turns out that particular wall, in that particular texture, by the mile.) Antonioni — and Art? What epithets do we set aside for Aeschylus, Aristophanes, et al.?

54

"Film — as Art? It's too soon to say, by several generations, I think. Of course film is presently an art form, with a small *a*. But then, so is pavement painting — and it's been around a lot longer. I'm not prepared to list two, twenty — or any — films to which schoolchildren will be exposed, say, two hundred years hence. They'll bloody well be absorbing the miracle of Shakespeare, though. And who knows? Absorption may be by then, literally the medium. The *Hamlet* pill; the *Titus Andronicus* suppository.

"Film itself, the physical commodity, already being superseded by video tape, with increasingly insubstantial substitutes already on the horizon, may actually cease to exist sooner than we think. A couple of hundred years from now man, in search of diversion, may simply settle back in some sort of electronic easy chair, adjust a pair of computerized stimuli to either side of his brain — and conjure up whatever pleasing fantasies occur to him at the moment. These, of course, will be instantaneously and faithfully transformed, by the magic of electronics, into a continuing flow of imagery projected upon a small screen which he will hold in his hand — as we now hold a book. At that point — what price Film Immortality?

"Bill Sampson's 'babying' of Margo — which struck you as becoming 'patronizing.' He doesn't really, you know. She wouldn't stand for it, not for a minute. 'Babying' the Margos of the theatre folk is a waste of effort. It's almost the first technique used in manipulating them professionally; very early on, stars learn that ass-kissing is almost always a form of negotiation."

There are remarkably few changes from first draft to final shooting script in the (only two) versions of the *All About Eve* screenplay. Mainly, it seemed to have been a matter of editing and refinement — from the former to the latter — culminating in what was still to be a very long (one hundred thirty-eight minutes) film for its era. The eliminated material merely elaborated points that the audience could quickly pick up from the subsequent action. The dialogue of the first draft, oddly enough, is almost as polished and precise as those aphoristic speeches heard from the screen. Such sure-handedness, at so early a stage, with what is usually the most reworked and rewritten aspect of any script, not only recalls Mankiewicz' early specialization as "dialoguist." It serves also to underscore his enduring high repute as a writer of what Vincent Canby describes as "urbane, sardonic comedies" and, to continue Canby's evaluation: "The sort of taste, intelligence and somewhat bitter humor I associate with Mr. Mankiewicz who, in real life, is one of America's most sophisticated, least folksy raconteurs." The quality — and, at times, overabundance — of Mankiewicz' dialogue has, in fact, led many critics to regard his talents as essentially those of a theatre playwright who has somehow diverted his writings from stage to screen. (Only recently, writing approvingly of Mankiewicz in *The Guardian*, Derek Malcolm wryly dubbed him: "Old Joe, the Talk Man.")

The major difference between the scripts and the released film version lies in the narrative structure. The dramatic construction of the scripts is more complex. There it is clear that we are getting a composite portrait of Eve, as seen from three different points of view — those of Addison, Karen, and Margo. Even the shooting script keeps cutting back to each of these three narrators at the Sarah Siddons banquet as each relinquishes one segment of the story, and another picks his up. The total effect was to be, according to Mankiewicz: "A composite mosaic-like structure in which several characters, while narrating their remembrances of still another, construct not only a portrait of the character in question but inadvertent self-portraits as well."

Another technique utilized by Mankiewicz in his final screenplay was the repetition of the same scene as witnessed from two different points of view. In the shooting script of *Eve*, this technique is used only once, but to great effect. In the sequence showing the party given by Margo for Bill Sampson's homecoming, Eve's speech about the meaning of applause ("Imagine, to know every night that different hundreds of people love you . . .") is presented to us first from Karen's point of view — and later from Margo's. From the scenes that precede each point of view (i.e., Karen's, followed by Margo's) we gain a clearer understanding of both women's reactions to Eve and of their subsequent behavior to her. Although the sequence was shot as written, it never reached the screen.

All About Eve is structurally an extremely elaborate use of one of the basic forms of film storytelling: the flashback. Anyone searching for a common narrative approach among Mankiewicz' films, as widely different in genre as they are, might begin by examining his use of this technique. The flashback and its advantages in characterizing human behavior — "summoning up not only the effect of the past upon the present, but also the degree to which the past *exists* in the present" — have made it Mankiewicz' favorite form of dramatic construction. *Somewhere in the Night* (1946) concerns an amnesiac's attempt to trace his lost identity; *Letter to Three Wives* (1949) recalls the marital memories of three women who are informed that one of their husbands is about to run away with another woman; *The Barefoot Contessa* (1954), which presents the director's "most un-

57

impeded" use of the "mosaic" construction, begins as a group of mourners gathers around actress Maria Vargas' grave and recalls, each in turn, Maria's tragic life. (Here, too, Mankiewicz utilizes the technique of repeating the same scene as different characters recall it, thus "providing a single narrative episode with varying dramatic connotations." This time, Mankiewicz having approval of the editing, the scenes in question remained in the released film.) *Suddenly, Last Summer* (1959), tells the story of a girl who has been severely traumatized by a past experience. (Gore Vidal and Tennessee Williams wrote the screenplay, based upon the latter's play.) It is worthy of note that here Mankiewicz utilizes, long before it became a fairly common film technique, the device of the "subliminal recall": the climactic scene in which the girl, Catherine, struggling to remember, manages to summon up to her memory only a flash or two of the past — and then loses it.

Mankiewicz' most ambitious, and hopefully "definitive," involvement with the flashback was to have been *Justine*, his adaptation of Lawrence Durrell's *The Alexandria Quartet.* He says of this unrealized project:

"It became necessary for·me to withdraw from *Justine*, and I consider that the greatest disappointment of my career. The fact that it was preceded by, and resulted from, the most humiliating experience of my career didn't help much, either. I was ecstatic about the film possibilities of the *Quartet*; within them lay the most difficult, but potentially the most gratifying, challenge I had ever faced as a writer-director. I had been working on it for many months (there are still, in my files, a couple of hundred pages of screenplay Fox never even requested to see) when I was urgently approached by Spyros Skouras and my (then) agent Charles Feldman. Would I suspend my work on *Justine* to take over a very

58

expensive, very sick movie Fox had just closed down in London? Mark you, they didn't hold a gun to my head — there was a very large amount of money involved — it was, on my part, knowingly an act of whoredom — I was handsomely paid. And, in the end, in turn, I paid. Most unhandsomely indeed.

"You see, I had solved the two major problems of incorporating all four volumes of the *Quartet* into one viable film-structure. (All four were, after all, essential components of Durrell's single entity. Not one was expendable. It was either all — or nothing. I haven't seen the film that eventuated, called *Justine,* but apparently, based upon what I've heard about it, they settled for nothing.) The problems were those of the two continua: the time continuum and that of narrative content. I had written an exhaustive, detailed screenplay-treatment. Just as with *All About Eve* and my other screenplays, this was the most difficult and time-consuming aspect of the entire project. Except that *Eve* and the others were as the New York *Daily News* crossword compared to Ximenes of the *London Observer.* Talk about 'mosaic' structuring; this was my answer to Daedalus and that simple little labyrinth he whipped up for the Minotaur.

"My screenplay-treatment was ridiculously long, I was well aware of that, but footage had not been my chief concern while structuring the film. Editing the treatment to a realistic length would not be easy, but certainly feasible; as a matter of fact, I was progressing nicely toward that end while writing my aborted first-draft screenplay. The treatment, however, did have one peculiarity that was probably considered outrageous: the content of it would be unintelligible to anyone who had not read all four volumes of *The Alexandria Quartet.* I placed a warning to that effect on its title page. This, of course, decimated the potential readership on the Twentieth

Century-Fox lot. At first-hand, I know of only one who did read it: young Richard Zanuck. He was most enthusiastic and, up to the bitter end (and I do mean bitter), encouraging and anxious for me to complete the project. I shall always wish him well.

"The other reader of my *Justine* screenplay treatment that I know about was Lawrence Durrell. I sat opposite him in a hotel room in Paris, keeping him from food and drink and even the toilet, until he had read it from start to finish. Larry expressed his delight; he was most congratulatory. I suppose, eventually, I shall have to make do with that much; not, after all, inconsiderable praise. But I do wish it had all been otherwise — and that I'd been able to finish *Justine*. I cannot help feeling that if ever I were to summon up enough talent to make a definitive film about anything, this would have been it — for me, at any rate — about a woman."

(The "humiliating experience" Mankiewicz refers to was, of course, *Cleopatra*, particularly its aftermath. This is the one film in his lengthy career which he steadfastly refuses even to refer to by name. Mankiewicz had conceived of *Cleopatra*, and wanted it so released, as two separate films, to play simultaneously in separate theatres, each to run about two hours and twenty minutes. The studio management refused even to consider this concept, and emasculated the footage — in particular, according to Mankiewicz, the performance of Richard Burton — into one film, lasting a little over four hours. It has since been hacked into varying shorter lengths. Almost, according to Mankiewicz, "to suit the whim of each individual theatre manager or projectionist. There's a good chance that it may wind up as a handful of the world's most expensive and beautifully photographed banjo picks."

60

At any rate, during the resultant brouhaha Mankiewicz was fired by the new management of Fox — and removed from any further connection with *Justine*.)

Mankiewicz is something of a rarity in American film in that for the most part he has written his screenplays in addition to directing them — a duality of responsibility that was rare in the assembly-line production methods of Hollywood. Long before he had the opportunity of putting the theory into practice (as far back as his MGM days, when he pleaded with L. B. Mayer for the chance to direct his screenplays), Mankiewicz was convinced that directing and writing for the screen were far from mutually exclusive:

"You know, one of the many frustrations which will increasingly confound our film historians will be a baffling inability not only to identify new techniques and concepts, but even to establish accurately when those presently employed were innovated — and by whom. The concept of *film auteur*, for example, presently the subject of so much intra-critical haggling (as if over the custody of an only child) — and which some believe to have been sired, in the late 50's, by the critical pantheon of the *Cahiers du Cinema*. Not so.

"Not even close. In 1946 Jean Benoit-Levy (*La Maternelle, Ballerina, et al.*) devoted much of his book, *The Art of the Motion Picture*, to a discussion of the nature, functions, and responsibilities of the *film auteur* — supplying, even, a rather ingenious chart which demonstrated his relationship to other components of the film-making process. Benoit-Levy used the epithet, *film auteur*, quite casually, as if it were common usage to describe a film maker so; certainly not as if it were a newly designated status, or one which he was originating. The following May (1947) I reviewed the book in a critical essay for *The Screen Writer* (a damn good film monthly published, at the time, by the Writers Guild of America). As the title of my essay I used its theme: '*Film Author! Film Author!*' Let me 'put into the record,' as presidents and lawyers say, a couple of paragraphs of what I wrote twenty-five years ago — presenting a point of view I consider equally valid today:

"I wrote then: 'An examination of the aforementioned chart (Benoit-Levy's, mentioned above) would indicate that an American equivalent of the *film author* would be our writer-director. That is, the *film author* works in immediate contact with a producer and his business organization; the original work from which he develops his script; his creative and technical associates, such as cameraman, set designer, cutter, composer, production staff, et al. However — and here is the very essence of his role in film making — the contribution of the *film author* is an uninterrupted process which begins with the development of the screenplay, and ends with the final editing of the film.'

"Next paragraph: 'Writing and directing moving pictures, then, are — and should be — the two components of that hyphenated entity, the *film author*. Put it as you will — that the direction of a screen play is the second half of the writer's work, or that the writing of a screen play is the first half of the director's work. The inescapable fact is that *a properly written screen play has in effect already been directed* — in his script, by the trained screen writer who has translated the visual and verbal concept of his film into descriptive movement, sound and spoken word. Thus the size of the image, its relationship to others, the point of view of the camera, the duration of the cut, the tempo of movement and speech, the nuances of interpretation, the need and nature of musical punctuation — in short, *the film* must unfold before the screen writer's eyes and in his mind as he writes. It seems to me to follow in natural creative sequence, then, for that same mind to direct the process by which this translation of his visual and verbal concept is realized upon the screen.' End of my quoting me, as of 1947.

"It shouldn't be stated that simplistically, of course. Especially against the background of commercial film-making in Hollywood when it was still getting away with the pretense of being an 'industry.' Would it interest you to know that the vast majority of American films turned out in the thirties and forties were shot by directors who were handed their scripts anywhere from two to ten days before the starting date? Scripts already cast from the studio stock company — and to be shot in standing sets? (Sets which were never 'struck,' simply re-dressed, then used over and over.) That, in most instances, the director never even met the writer or writers? That the writer or writers, halfway through other assignments by now, probably at other studios, rarely knew to what extent — if any — the director understood, or agreed, with the concept they had so painstakingly committed to paper? I remember writing in my foreword to the original hardbound edition of *All About Eve* [Random House, 1951]: 'Inasmuch as his filmscript may be on the stage many months after he has written it, and inasmuch as he may be not only mentally but geographically remote from it, the writer's voluminous technical exhortations act sometimes within his filmscript as a sort of last testament — as a plea, by remote control, for a voice in what goes on the screen, and how it gets there.'

"I think it's important that I define, getting back to my

concept of *film author,* what I meant by screenwriter. I did *not* mean just any member in good standing of the Writers Guild. Nor, by screenwriting, did I mean only the particular talent to fit the proper word to the dramatic point, mood, or emotion. I cannot think of a topflight director — from Griffith through Lubitsch up to and including Fellini — who was not also, in a very true sense, a topflight screenwriter. That they by themselves could not actually commit the words to paper was, and is, relatively unimportant. What is important is that the shooting script must faithfully represent the one concept of whatever individual talent guides and controls the making of the film. True, the professional writers with whom they would work in close collaboration throughout the building of the script undoubtedly contributed a great deal of their own — but always within the concept of the dominative creator. Similarly, the professional cinematographer and other creative talents would thereafter also contribute much of their own — this time, to the second half of the *film author*'s work.

"Still, there are always those craftsmen, varying in both talent and basic approach to film-making, writer or director, who — for reasons of personal temperament or simple disinterest — remain seemingly content to perform only their designated half of the *film author*'s function. There are good writers who are satisfied with the contributive participation I've just described. Also hack writers who 'knock out' the screenplays, hack directors who carry out the directing. These two categories make most of the movies 'turned out' in the world. That dichotomy works, perhaps, for television. Television, after all, demands nothing more than precisely timed driblets of distraction between advertisements. Film can't survive such dichotomy. A screenplay just might happen to be

64

good. If it is, then implicitly a pattern of direction, a condition of having-already-been-directed is one of its major assets. For a director simply to 'shoot the script' is, in effect, to superimpose a second direction upon an already existent one. That's obviously destructive. Writing film and directing film are not, and should not be, separate and mutually exclusive functions."

There is no such superimposition in the direction of the script of *All About Eve*. While the shooting script is not a blueprint of camera movements nor detailed editing instructions for the cutting room ("The privilege of directing my own scripts," Mankiewicz has written, "has enabled me to use far less technical terminology than is usual."), it is most explicit as to directorial business and ambience, all of which are realized in the completed film. After I had seen the film for the umpteenth time, I mentioned several bits that I hadn't remembered from a recent reading of the screenplay. Mankiewicz answered:

"I think you'll find those in the script. Certainly, many details and nuances of characterization emerge from discussion and rehearsal with talented actors. But by and large, major deviations are rarely improvements when arrived at under pressure, off-the-cuff. One of the many advantages of being able to write your own shooting script is the happy fact that it provides not only an opportunity to work out interpretative problems leisurely and away from that pressure of being on the stage, under the gun — but also the luxury of committing most of the solutions to paper, within the script itself."

I double-checked Mankiewicz' screenplay to see whether the bits I hadn't remembered were there or not. *Mea culpa.*

65

III

After finishing the script, Mankiewicz began his "assignment as director" at the beginning of April 1950. His first concern was the pre-production planning of the film: conferences concerning costumes, sets, final casting, budgeting, and the preparation of a shooting schedule. *All About Eve* was given a forty-day shooting period; as soon as actual production began, this was to prove unrealistically optimistic. Though it finished over schedule, the film was still made in an astonishingly short length of time. Mankiewicz' first rough cut was delivered on June 24 (the date on which his "assignment as director" terminated). According to Fox records, the film cost $1,400,000 ($500,000 of which went to cover cast salaries); this sounds exceedingly modest in the light of today's production costs, but at that time, was by no means inexpensive.

All About Eve may seem tame today, but in 1950 much of its dialogue and some of its situations for the time were very daring indeed. At that time it was obligatory to have scripts approved by the production code office. Like most companies, Twentieth Century-Fox employed their own experts to forewarn them of any trouble areas that might develop when the script was submitted. In a memo dated April 5, Colonel Jason Joy, Fox's liaison officer to Joseph Breen, who was chief administrator of the production code, warned Darryl F. Zanuck of the problems that might lie ahead. Among them were the following, gleaned from Col. Joy's memorandum to both Zanuck and Mankiewicz:

66

1. Re Margo's speech in the first dressing room scene, "Ah don' understand about all these plays about sex-stahved Suth'n women — sex is one thing we was nevah stahved for in the South!" Col. Joy felt that it might be expedient to change "sex-stahved" to "love-stahved." Mankiewicz, answering this memo on April 6, stoically agreed to this change.

2. Re Margo's comment later on in the same scene, "You know, I can remember plays about women — even from the South — where it never even occurred to them whether they wanted to marry their fathers more than their brothers," Colonel Joy thought a happier turn of phrase might be "whether they had a fixation for their fathers or their brothers." Mankiewicz answered, "I do not like Jason's substitution of 'fixation' for 'marry' in Margo's teasing line about Lloyd's plays. I cannot imagine even censors objecting to the line as it is now written — delivered in a light, ribbing tone. The proper word, in any case, would be 'screw.' "

3. Re a stage direction which asks Birdie to run the water in Margo's bathroom, Col. Joy remarks enigmatically, "The bathroom, will, of course, be all right." Mankiewicz enlightens us to the meaning of this delicate reference by commenting, "By my Oscars, I promise to show no indication of a toilet. Has it ever occurred to Joe Breen that the rest of the world must be convinced by now that Americans never relieve themselves?"

4. Re Birdie's line, "Everything but the bloodhounds snappin' at her rear end," Joy remarks encouragingly, "Insomuch as Birdie's line is at the end of the shot, perhaps you can let it go the way it is and clip off 'rear end' if we have to, although I don't think we will." Mankiewicz is obviously beginning to lose his temper: "The word *should* be 'arse.' What do you suggest we substitute for 'rear end?' 'Backside?'

'Butt?' What would you think of 'snappin' at her transmission?' "

5. Re the line "Meet me in the ladies' room," Col. Joy wondered, "If you think that changing 'ladies' room' to 'powder room' would not hurt the following speech of Bill Sampson (referring to Eve, he says, 'I understand she is now the understudy in there.'), I think you would like to do it." Mankiewicz, however, didn't like: "Changing 'ladies' room' to 'powder room' is not only childish but will most certainly hurt Bill's comment. 'Understudy' refers to ladies and not to 'powder.' "

There was, however, a positive side even to Hollywood's abject capitulation to any and all censorship demands. Says Mankiewicz:

"The bluenosed restrictions of the time were not just crackbrained (for many years I treasured a memorandum, issued in all seriousness by the Will Hays Office, banning the udders from the cows in the Mickey Mouse cartoons); they were iniquitous, of course, and suppressive. Still, there they were. And you worked according to them — or you didn't work. Those same 'industry' leaders who had been quick to remove Jewish names from the credits of movies they kept selling Nazi Germany until Hitler threw them out, were not about to do battle with the censorship boards and Catholic Church here at home.

"The challenge facing the creative craftsman was to come up with ways in which he could 'intimate' 'suggestions' of 'implications' of 'allusions' to subject matter and/or human behavior he was forbidden either to describe or to show. For both the screenwriter and director, this put a premium on, above all, ingenuity. Thus the techniques of 'indirection,' the nuances within both dialogue and performance, obliqueness

68

of narrative structure and intent flourished during those years of Procrustean censorship, in my opinion, as never before or since in the American film. Lubitsch, for example, could induce more enjoyable and provocative sexual excitement by his direction of a fully dressed young woman deciding whether or not to open a bedroom door — than any one of, or combination of, the most explicit hand-held full-screen close-ups of intertwined genitals presently before the public eye."

Mankiewicz' greatest problems during the pre-production period were caused by casting. Darryl F. Zanuck, head of the Twentieth Century-Fox Studio at the time, had decided personally to produce *All About Eve* after reading Mankiewicz' first-draft screenplay. His first choices for the roles of Margo, Eve, and Addison DeWitt were: Marlene Dietrich, Jeanne Crain, and José Ferrer. Mankiewicz objected strenuously to two of those choices. He remembers, "I was, and am, a great admirer of Marlene. But from what I knew of her work and equipment as an actress, I simply could not visualize — or 'hear' — her as a possible Margo." Claudette Colbert was Mankiewicz' first choice for the role and she was signed for it in February 1950.

Jeanne Crain was a favorite of Zanuck and the exhibitors of the period. Mankiewicz, however, had not been happy with her performance in *A Letter to Three Wives*. (He was to use her again, his objections overruled, in *People Will Talk*). "It was probably my fault," he emphasizes, "but I could only rarely escape the feeling that Jeanne was, somehow, a visitor to the set. She worked hard. Too hard at times, I think, in response to my demands, as if trying to compensate by sheer exertion for what I believe must have been an absence of emotional involvement with acting. I wouldn't think she took the role home with her at night; she would assume it, rather, every morning with her wardrobe change for the day. I remember Jeanne Crain as a very pleasant, very shy, and very devout young woman, mother, and wife whose husband was doing very well in some business. She was one of the few whose presence among the theatre-folk I have never fully understood."

Zanuck yielded this time to his plea that he could not elicit from Jeanne Crain the degree of "bitch virtuosity" needed for the proper playing of Eve — and approved Mankiewicz' suggestion of Anne Baxter, also under contract to the studio at the time. Celeste Holm, still another contract player, was approved for Karen, a part for which the actress was ideally suited. Mankiewicz does not now remember how José Ferrer was replaced in the role of Addison by George Sanders.

There had never been any doubt as to the casting of Birdie Coonan, Margo's dresser/companion (and another of Mankiewicz' *alter ego* commentators). "Birdie was written for only Thelma Ritter," Mankiewicz confirms. "I adored her. Thelma was that rare performing talent which the writer and/or director must treasure as a fiddler would a Stradivarius. Prior to *A Letter to Three Wives* she had appeared on the screen only in a 'bit' — a memorable 'bit,' to be sure — for George Seaton in *Miracle on 34th Street*. I shall always be proud of my share in creating her image for the film audience — and in providing that audience for her. Thelma Ritter was one of the last of, by now, an almost extinct species in our theatrical ecology: the great character comedienne."

Shortly before the picture was to begin production, Claudette Colbert had an accident in which she severely wrenched her back and as a result was forced to withdraw from the film. The hurried search began for another leading lady. Mankiewicz' second choice had always been Gertrude Lawrence. She had read his screenplay treatment and liked it enormously.

"However," says Mankiewicz, "'submitting the actual screenplay to her suddenly became a highly complicated procedure. To this day, I don't know whether Gertie ever did read it; I'm quite sure that if she had, she would have crawled to California to play it. Somehow, a protocol of approach to Miss Lawrence had come into being. All scripts were first to be submitted to, and approved by, her lawyer, the redoubtable Fanny Holtzman (celebrated for having represented the Yussoupov family in its eminently successful libel suit against MGM over *Rasputin and the Empress*). Miss (Mrs.?) Holtzman read the screenplay and called me at home to say she found it very good. There were only two changes she would insist upon: 1) The drunk scenes would have to be eliminated. It would be preferable, in fact, if Miss Lawrence neither drank nor smoked at all on the screen. 2) During the party sequence, the pianist was not to play 'Liebestraum.' Instead, he would accompany Miss Lawrence as she sang a torch song about Bill. (Something I thought Helen Morgan had already done, rather successfully.) Since my own lawyer had always admonished me to respond to other lawyers with either 'yes' or 'no' and urged me to 'keep the witty ripostes for when you're shaving' — I said nothing but 'no'. And that's how Gertrude Lawrence did not play Margo Channing."

There was one very good reason why Bette Davis had never been offered the part: throughout that period she was filming *Payment on Demand* and was therefore considered hopelessly unavailable. But now that Miss Colbert's illness had delayed the start of *Eve*, Darryl Zanuck submitted the script to Miss Davis on the off chance that the two schedules might fit. *Payment* actually finished shooting no more than two weeks prior to the new "must" starting date of *All About Eve*. Miss Davis read the screenplay, liked it so much that she agreed to forgo any vacation between films, and launched forthwith into wardrobe tests.

The casting of Davis had a memorable effect on the film. It also raised, and still raises, the question of whether Mankiewicz had, as has often been maintained, Tallulah Bankhead in mind when he created Margo — or whether the similarity emerged only from Bette Davis' performance of the role. Mankiewicz smiled when I put the question to him:

"I've always told the truth about that, and nobody has ever quite believed me. I remember being asked the same question, by somebody in the audience, at the time I received the New York Film Critics Award for directing. I answered truthfully then, too. I said that I was happy to have the opportunity of revealing, at long last, who the archetype for Margo Channing had been. That it had been none other than Peg Woffington.* Late, very late, of Old Drury Lane . . .

"Peg Woffington. I think I've read everything written about her, fact and gossip. Woffington was/is Margo Channing. From her talent and triumphs on stage to her personal and private torments off. She was also Bette Davis. Also Mrs. Bellamy, Maggie Smith and Isabella Andreini, Mrs. Siddons and Joan Crawford, Modjeska, both Molière's wife

---

* Peg Woffington was one of the great actresses and beauties of the eighteenth-century English theatre. Offstage, she was notorious for her amours (a particularly tempestuous one with David Garrick); on stage, for her brilliant performance and feuds with her arch-rival, Mrs. Bellamy.

and his mistress, Jessica Tandy, Laurette Taylor and Rachel, Zoe Caldwell, Sybil Thorndike and, yes, Tallulah. Every woman for whom acting was identical with existence. Glorious broads, all of them, baffling and sad and exciting, and they've made living in this world a richer experience ever since (in Italy, of all places) they first liberated woman's right to play a woman. Don't hold me to that list; I've left out hundreds. Woffington, to me, was their prototype, all of them. And all of them in part are Margo Channing, I hope. Performing women. I won't stop being fascinated and terrified by them; I won't stop thinking and learning and writing about them until I die."

According to Mankiewicz, it never occurred to either Bette Davis or him that there was any particular "Bankhead quality" about Margo. The surface resemblances came about through happenstance. On the night before Davis arrived on the set in San Francisco, "in the course of a pointed discussion about domestic problems," she had burst a tiny blood vessel in her throat. Throat specialists were consulted and they advised that the actress could work without danger to her health. But the accident had provided an added huskiness to her voice, which recorded surprisingly like Bankhead's very individual bourbon contralto. And as Mankiewicz warned Miss Davis: once she spoke the first words in her new register, the die was cast. She would have to maintain it throughout the film. And so she did. As for the shoulder-length mop of hair, Mankiewicz remembers that it was simply an expedient choice: Miss Davis had worn it before; it was attractive and "Margo-like," easy to keep in place without undue fuss.

Mankiewicz recalls that some time after the film was released, he was approached by a mutual friend of his and

Claudette Colbert's who asked the director, "What the hell made you ever think that Claudette could have played Margo Channing?" I interrupted to say that I thought a lot of people wondered the same thing. Mankiewicz's reply:

"When *All About Eve* was released there was quite a hullabaloo concerning it as a *film à clef* about Tallulah Bankhead. Tallulah, understandably enough, did little to dispel the assumption; on the contrary, she exploited it to the hilt with great skill and gusto. (Even to the extent of asserting that I had visited the set of *A Royal Scandal*, back in 1945, to study her mannerisms. I visited the set, true. But I was studying Lubitsch, not Bankhead.) At any rate, what with all the public brouhaha, Tallulah's star re-achieved a certain amount of ascendancy. She wound up with a popular ninety-minute radio program called *The Big Show*, of which the basic joke was an imaginary Davis–Bankhead feud. (Imaginary show biz 'feuds,' à la Jack Benny–Fred Allen, were in vogue at the time.) No, she did all right for herself, did Talloo. The performance of Bette Davis provided Miss Bankhead with quite a run.

"And therein lay my answer to Claudette's and my friend — and to you: 'If Claudette had played Margo Channing,' I told him, 'either Ina Claire or Lynn Fontanne, if so inclined, might well have had a ninety-minute radio program.' I'm not sure he understood my analogy — he was a 'private person' — but it should be perfectly clear to anyone who has ever written, acted, or directed professionally. Both Bette and Claudette are greatly talented and resourceful actresses, equally proficient in the art of utilizing their superb equipment — yet not at all alike, necessarily, in either the nature of that equipment or their approach to the same role.

"Of course Claudette could have played the part. Beautifully. If she had, Margo would simply have emerged on a different plateau of performance. Possibly no more effective, but certainly no less. The same dramatic points would have been made; their sum total the same. The difference would lie in the orchestration, if you will — the utilization, as I've said, of different equipment, different instrumentation, different emotional components within each actress. One would use ice instead of heat; the foil could replace the karate chop; an increasingly bitchy, ever more piss-elegant drunk would equate with the boozy slugger-from-the-toe; unhappiness is no whit happier if examined from the intellect rather than the gut — and here I go, belaboring the obvious again. In just one season we've had three very exciting, very different Hedda Gablers (Maggie Smith, Claire Bloom, Irene Worth) with one thing in common — *Hedda Gabler*. There is no one way to play a properly written role, any more than there is only one actress for that role. Otherwise, the art of interpretation would require little talent indeed — and the director's contribution would be minimal. Traffic cops would suffice."

For the minor role of Miss Caswell, Mankiewicz' choice was Marilyn Monroe. She had previously been under contract to Fox for two or three years, as a member of the studio "stock company." (As Mankiewicz describes the services she was required to perform, they had little to do with acting. "For the most part she auditioned a great deal, late afternoons, in executive offices. She also functioned agreeably as a companion for corporative elder statesmen visiting from the east, and on hostess committees for sales conventions. Occasionally, she was squeezed into old Betty Grable costumes and used as a dress extra or for unimportant bits in some films.") Marilyn Monroe was dropped by Fox, as a

75

contract player, about two years before the casting of *All About Eve* took place. Some of what Mankiewicz had to relate about her return to the studio:

"One of the most irritating aspects of the vast amount of crap that has been thrown up into print about Marilyn, apart from its sickening mawkishness, is its inaccuracy. Particularly as it relates to her second start at Fox, and her subsequent trip to the Hollywood moon. Let me testify at once that while I was instrumental in getting her the part of Miss Caswell, I did not make a star of Marilyn Monroe. No individual, to the best of my pretty extensive knowledge, ever made a star. That is a power and privilege restricted only to the unfathomable, improbable, and altogether unworthy authority known as the Mass Audience. The so-called Hollywood 'Star-Makers' have invariably been crap-shooters with other men's money; to mix my metaphors, after betting every horse in the race they would hold up only the winning ticket. Louis B. Mayer, for one, did exactly that.

"To get back to Marilyn and *Eve* and Fox. Let me state one fact quite simply: the only person importantly associated with *All About Eve* with no supportable claim whatsoever to having brought her back to Twentieth Century-Fox (except, of course, his ultimate reluctant approval, which was legally necessary) was Darryl F. Zanuck. Upon my proposal of her name his opposition was instantaneous, vehement and — based upon her earlier 'career' at the studio — possibly justifiable. Nor, I must add, was my championship of her equally vehement and adamant. True, I thought she'd be good for the role. I'd interviewed some eight or ten young actresses for the part, all of them of equal physical endowment and professional prowess — I believe Sheree North was one — and I felt Marilyn had the edge. There was a breath-

76

lessness and sort of glued-on innocence about her that I found appealing — and she had done a good job for John Huston in *The Asphalt Jungle*. Still, I wasn't about to tear up my contract and stomp out if she didn't get the part.

"As it turned out, I didn't have to. Standing my ground was made easier for me because my endorsement of Marilyn was merely supportive to the major force that desperately wanted her in my film. That major force was a very important agent named Johnny Hyde — at the time certainly no less than the #2 or #3 power at William Morris. Like most great agents, he was a tiny man. (There's a book there, too; or maybe just a minor address at some psychoanalytic congress.) Johnny Hyde was also a very honest and a very gentle man. He was also deeply in love with Marilyn. And more than anyone in her life, I think, provided for her something akin to an honest *ego* of her own; he respected her. Permitting her, in turn, to acquire a certain amount of self-respect. After Johnny died — suddenly, not too long afterwards — it has always seemed to me that Marilyn, despite all of the intellectual and cultural and personality flurries, gave up on herself. The biographers of Monroe, when they mention him at all, are seemingly overinfluenced by the unhappy fact that he never hit a ball out of Yankee Stadium, never even wrote a play.

"It was Johnny Hyde who brought Marilyn to me for Miss Caswell. It had been six months or more since *Asphalt Jungle*; he knew the importance of momentum to any career. He knew especially the importance to Marilyn, for herself, to work in an important film. He haunted my office. And once I'd said 'yes' — more than anyone, it was Johnny Hyde who fought the good fight to break down the considerable resistance to her return to Twentieth Century-Fox. On March

27, 1950, Marilyn Monroe was signed for five hundred dollars a week — on a one-week guarantee. I imagine there was appended to it the usual very long-term contract, at the option of the studio. It was an enormously profitable one for Fox, and lasted until she took her life."

When Mankiewicz speaks about Marilyn Monroe, there is tenderness and a protective quality in his voice: "There is one particular remembrance I have of Marilyn which I think tells a great deal about her at the time. One day on the set — we were shooting the party sequence — she walked by me, carrying a thin book. Had she been carrying a thin snake, I would have thought nothing of it. But a book. I called her over and asked what she was reading. She didn't say; she just handed it to me. It was Rainer Maria Rilke's *Letters to a Young Poet.* I'd have been less taken aback to come upon Herr Rilke studying a Marilyn Monroe nude calendar.

"I asked Marilyn if she knew who he was. She shook her head. 'No. Who is he?' I told her that Rilke had been a German poet, that he was dead, that I myself had read less of him and knew less about him than I should — and asked her how the hell she came to be reading him at all, much less that particular work of his. Had somebody recommended it to her? Again, a shake of her head: 'No. Nobody. You see, in my whole life I haven't read hardly anything at all. I don't know how to catch up. I don't know where to begin. So what I do is, every now and then I go into the Pickwick (a bookshop on Hollywood Boulevard, one of the very few in the entire City of the Angels which exists independent of being a required adjunct to an institution of learning) and just look around. I leaf through some books, and when I read something that interests me — I buy the book. So last night I bought this one. Is that wrong?' No, I told her, that

78

was far from wrong. That, in fact, it was the best possible way for anyone to choose what to read. She was not accustomed to being told she was doing anything right. She smiled proudly and moved on. The next day Marilyn sent me a copy of *Letters to a Young Poet*. I have yet to read it.

"I thought of her, then, as the loneliest person I had ever known. Throughout our location period in San Francisco, perhaps two or three weeks, Marilyn would be spotted at one restaurant or another dining alone. Or drinking alone. We'd always ask her to join us, and she would, and seemed pleased, but somehow she never understood or accepted our unspoken assumption that she was one of us. She remained alone. She was not a loner. She was just plain *alone*."

IV

Production began at the Curran Theatre in San Francisco on April 15, 1950. It soon became evident that the time allotted for the sequences to be shot in the theatre had been over-optimistically estimated; Mankiewicz fell behind schedule. The usual 'catch-up' harassment from the studio production office ensued.

"Nothing more accurately reflects the assembly-line approach to moviemaking which then prevailed," says Mankiewicz, "than the process by which shooting schedules were arrived at. And which still prevails, in general. A film script, to a studio production office, is a mathematical something. It consists of a specific number of pages which are to be committed to film in a specified number of days. The daily production reports, handed in every evening by the script girl, never refer to the difficulty or sensitivity of the day's

79

work; she is required to stick to the factory facts, ma'am. How many pages has the director knocked off; how much estimated (her estimate) assembled film time has been completed. The former determines the amount of pressure to be put on the director to catch up. The latter (estimated film time), if running long, will usually lead to suggested — and sometimes enforced — eliminations from the script. (John Ford was once being harangued, while shooting, by a Fox production manager — one of the Wurtzels, probably. It seems that Jack was three or four days behind — and did he really need such-and-such a sequence — and how was he gonna catch up — and Mr. Zanuck was personally getting upset — and so forth. Jack just sat behind his dark glasses and listened, sucking at his pipe. Finally he reached for the script, yanked out a random handful of pages, and tossed them at the Wurtzel. 'I am now back on schedule,' said Jack. 'Get the hell off my set.')

"Directors, at the time, were rated — and the ratings confidentially interchanged by studio production departments — as 'fast' or 'slow,' based upon their past performances. One would be 'good for five or six pages a day'; another, 'two and a half, if you're lucky.' Woody (W. S.) Van Dyke was MGM's pride and joy; no matter what the schedule, he'd invariably wind up a week under. A lot of it couldn't be cut together, or wouldn't match, or Joan Crawford's right eye would be offscreen — and just as invariably, there'd be a week of retakes for every week he'd finished ahead. He shot *San Francisco* in forty-six days, and there were fifty-four days of retakes.

"Lloyd Bacon was another favorite of the production offices. If Lloyd had his camera set up in the corner of a living room, say, he'd shoot everything that could conceivably be played in that corner throughout the entire script — in that same set-up. First, everything that called for day lighting; then everything lit for night. He figured it was quicker to change wardrobe than camera set-ups. He demanded very little from his actors; as soon as he'd yelled 'Cut!' he'd turn to his script girl and ask 'Did they get the titles right?' If she answered in the affirmative, he'd say 'Print it. What else happens here?' Lloyd Bacon never referred to dialogue as anything other than 'titles.'

"They were the golden boys of the major studios. Variants of Woody and Lloyd constituted a majority of the directors under term contract; they made most of the films of the thirties and forties. No, the enormous amount of retakes didn't bother the studio bosses. You see, there were no overhead charges applied to retakes. Which made for cheaper overall production cost. Which is just what the fake cockamaimy 'industry' wanted: 'product' short enough to be run seven or eight times a day, 'turned out' as inexpensively as possible and fed, at the rate of one a week or better, to the *real* Minotaur of the American film (*and* the British, *and* the Italian, *and* the French, and so forth), the retail 'outlet.' The exhibitor.

"The exhibitor — the movie-theatre owner — has always pocketed the lion's share of what the public pays to see a film. Regularly, in *Variety* — that highly inaccurate 'bible of show biz' — you will read figures purporting to be the box-office 'grosses' of films. The word 'gross' is a deliberate (not *Variety*'s, but they go along with it) misdefinition. *Nobody* except the exhibitor has ever had a share of the box-office gross of any film ever made. Quite a statement? I'll compound the heresy. I'll wager that nobody has ever *known* the box-office gross of any film ever made. How much has, let's say,

81

Gone with the Wind been reputed to have 'grossed'? Seventy or eighty million dollars, roughly? That figure, or whatever the stipulated figure is, represents about one-third of what the public paid at the box office to see the film. The other two-thirds has stuck to the sticky fingers of the real-estate operators who owned the theatres attached to those box offices — and who call themselves 'showmen.' The approximate one-third is what they've reluctantly passed on to the distributors of the film. That one-third is blithely called the 'gross.' But it is not a gross. It is very much a 'net.'

"How the distributor in turn then lops off a basic 30-50% of that so-called 'gross,' which is really a net — in addition to a variety of charges, interests, fees, and other larcenies which would embarrass Ebenezer Scrooge — before he, yelping with pain, hands over a reluctant buck to the actual film maker — that's a whole different book.

"Still not clear? Let's assume that you have never produced a play on Broadway. That your grandmother has never written a play — and your grandfather has never starred in one. But suddenly your grandmother does write a play. And you decide to produce it, starring your grandfather. You've raised the money. You don't want to put it on in a cellar; for some reason you want a Broadway theatre. So you go to the Shuberts; you've heard they control a lot of them. Now let's say the Shuberts read your grandmother's play and think it stinks. They've never heard of you as a producer — and are not impressed by the box-office appeal of your grandfather. Still, you have got the money — and they have an empty theatre or two. Remember, you're dealing with the Shuberts — reputedly, the toughest of the tough. They lay it on the line. You can have a theatre, they say — but on their most stringent terms. Take it or leave it. Of what the public pays at the box office to see your play — the only honest definition of gross — they get 35% and you get 65%. You gulp — and take it. That worst deal the Shuberts can hand out is better than the best any film exhibitor is prepared to offer for nine-tenths of the movies he runs through his out-of-focus projection machines. And don't forget, the Shubert theatres — a lot of them — are dark for many months in the year. Yet it is written — on some Tablet, on some Mount — that the projection machines of America, for twelve hours (or more) a day and for seven days of the week, must never stop running.

"Remember the great Hollywood labor scandals of the mid-forties? Willie Bioff and George Browne? The total capitulation of the studio heads, their frantic payoffs, anything to avoid that threatened strike? It wasn't the carpenters or electricians the moguls wanted to keep from striking. Disconcerting as it is to contemplate, they plus the Screen Actors Guild plus the Writers Guild of America plus the Directors Guild of America could walk out together, arm in arm — and the 'product' would still 'somehow' be fabricated. No, there is only one union — and one union alone — of which the 'film industry' lives in terror. If the Projectionists of America were to strike — if the Projection Machines of America were to stop for so much as a week or a month — that monolithic 'industry'-exhibitor superstructure which has controlled and stifled the American film for as long as I can remember, would collapse like a stabbed soufflé.

"Odd, isn't it? Of all the troubled unions that come to mind, and considering the widespread dissatisfaction and unrest within labor ranks generally — the projectionists, to my knowledge, have never struck. It's good to know they're being kept happy in their work. There's no boss like a terrified boss.

"Anyhow. Where was I — with *Eve*? In San Francisco,

two or three days behind schedule after a couple of weeks of shooting. The memos and calls from the studio were getting less and less understanding — and more and more pointed about what the hell was I up to. You must understand also about studio production offices, their unshakable conviction that whenever a director left the actual studio confines with his company — it became his avowed purpose to squander recklessly the studio's resources.

"Also, my own production office 'rating' was neither 'fast' nor 'slow'; I belonged to a third classification which irritated the shit out of production managers. The 'can't-figure-him' type of director. This meant, usually, that the director was either unpredictable in his shooting methodry or that he was (in their opinion) over-meticulous in certain aspects of his work. It might be the number of takes, the superfluity (in their opinion) of camera angles, a propensity for mid-rehearsal setup changes, and so on. That type had to be 'handled,' 'pressured,' whatever his idiosyncrasy. In my case, it was the actor's performance. That has always been, and remains, the one component of film-making with which I find myself least able to compromise. In many a production office I've been, and remain, snarlingly categorized as a 'perfectionist.' I'm not. If I were, I'd still be rehearsing the first scene of the first film I ever made.

"And so, in San Francisco, the pressure was on. Lubitsch once said to me, concerning the director's general approach to his film, that by and large he should make it for himself, as a film *he* would buy a ticket to see — and then pray for millions of people to agree with him. That seems pretty self-evident. But it wasn't all that easy to accomplish back then, when the studio–director relationship was too often one of continual petty harassment. It could result too often in continuing small compromises which would turn out, in the end, to have been very damaging, indeed. 'Perfectionist' or not, I've made my share of them. More than my share.

"A touch of clairvoyance would have come in handy. Thus, when that memo or phone call came in asking whether you couldn't shoot the reverse back in the studio — or why must the scene be played so that the whole auditorium has to be lit — or whatever — you could yell: 'Get off my back! This film is going to win fourteen Academy Award nominations; five of the actors will be nominated; it will win every frigging Best of the Year Award from the American and British Academies to the New York Critics; from Cannes to Japan, Cuba, points East and West — so shove the three days I'm behind schedule!' But you're never clairvoyant, you don't yell those things — you have no way of knowing, actually, that the film won't wind up on its ass. So you go right on, functioning as you always have. You've done your best on the hits; you've done your best on the flops, too. In the end, the outcome seems to depend upon a magical intangible that no one has ever been able to define — much less control. I wouldn't have it any other way. That intangible is what the theatre is all about."

Throughout the entire shooting period, Mankiewicz must have succeeded in keeping the behind-the-scene production pressures from affecting his company of players on the set. As witness the oft-repeated testimony of all concerned to the effect that the making of the film was, for each, a memorably gratifying professional experience. Even though Mankiewicz is noted for his firm hand with so-called 'star temperament,' it should be pointed out that, in addition to the inevitable

85

tensions that can arise among important actors playing essentially competitive roles, three of his leading ladies had already won Academy Awards* and the fourth was an accomplished scene-stealer whose role had been hand-tailored to her talents.

Actually, according to Mankiewicz, the only moment he experienced of even apprehension occurred before the filming of *All About Eve* began. No sooner was it announced in the trade press that Bette Davis was to play Margo Channing, than Mankiewicz received phone calls from two or three directors who were his friends and who had worked with the actress in the past. To a man, they predicted a Davis–Mankiewicz head-on clash that could end only in disaster. The director grinned as he recalled the incident:

"I remember most vividly Eddie Goulding's** prophecy of doom and destruction. 'Dear boy,' moaned Eddie. 'Have you gone mad? This woman will destroy you, she will grind you down to a fine powder and blow you away. You are a writer, dear boy. She will come to the stage with a thick pad of long yellow paper. And pencils. She will write. And then she, not you, will direct. Mark my words.' The others weren't as vehement as Eddie (I assumed they'd merely been scratched whereas he might still have an open wound or two) — but I did mark his words and prepared for the worst. Always a good thing to prepare for, among theatre-folk.

"Instead of the worst, of course, what eventuated was the very best — another turn of events not uncommon to theatri-

* Bette Davis: 1935 and 1938; Anne Baxter: 1946; Celeste Holm: 1947.

** Edmund Goulding directed Miss Davis in four films: *That Certain Woman* (1937), *Dark Victory* (1939), *The Old Maid* (1939), and *The Great Lie* (1941). On the last film, it is a Hollywood legend that Miss Davis and her co-star, Mary Astor, rewrote the script daily.

86

cal experience. Working with Bette was, it goes without saying, from the first day to regrettably our last, an experience as happy and rewarding as any I have ever known. Barring grand opera, I can think of nothing beyond her range. She's intelligent, instinctive, vital, sensitive — and, above all, a superbly equipped professional actress who does her job responsibly and honestly. To this day I regret deeply that I hadn't worked with her before *Eve* — and that I haven't since.

"Still, that first day of shooting, I was marking Eddie Goulding's words. I had my antennae deployed to pick up possible storm warnings. Miss Davis arrived on the set, fully dressed and made up, at least a quarter of an hour before she'd been called. She carried nothing but her copy of my script. A pleasant 'good morning,' and she sat in her chair. I watched for her to 'case' my provisional camera placement and the rough lighting of the set. (Not at all uncommon, then. Norma Shearer knew her 'key' light as Dr. De Bakey knows the human heart. Rex Harrison — jokingly, of course — would occasionally say 'Good morning, old cock' to the lens. 'If you cahn't see the lens, the lens cahn't see you' was his credo.) Bette didn't even glance at the set; she lit a cigarette and opened the script — not, I noticed at once, to the scene we were doing that first morning.

"I called rehearsal. I know I can't generate any suspense in describing the day, so why try? Bette was letter-perfect. She was syllable-perfect. There was no fumbling for my words; they'd become hers — as Margo Channing. The director's dream: the prepared actress. It shouldn't be, really; it's a prerequisite, after all. Unless the actor is prepared, the director cannot truly function — nor, for that matter, can the actor. Acting otherwise becomes simply a struggle to articulate basic content. Directing becomes a tense concentration on progress, at the expense of performance.

("Let me interpose quickly, here, that Bette's professional attributes were not unique within the *Eve* company. Without exception, the entire cast was no less conscientious. It was a rare treat, believe me, even then — a time when the inarticulate had not yet, as now, replaced the coherent. I suppose over the years I've been luckier than most directors in having had responsible acting talent to work with — but never more fortunate than in *All About Eve*.)

"To return to those first few shooting days. The gloomy predictions of Goulding and the others hung on a bit, like the leftover of a head cold — but it soon became evident that either they had been wrong about Bette Davis or I was working with an imposter. So one afternoon, sitting around between set-ups and without identifying any of the Cassandras by name (although Eddie, I must say, had maintained bravely, 'and you may quote me, dear boy'), I told Bette about the forewarnings I'd received, about my first-day apprehensions. And that where I'd been led to expect Lady Macbeth — in her place had arrived Portia. Was it a rib? A put-on of some kind? Or what? Bette snorted. That inimitable Davis snort. Then she laughed. Her snort and her laugh should both be protected by copyright. I can't quote her reply exactly, of course, but in content it was roughly as follows:

"Said Bette: 'I am neither Lady Macbeth nor Portia; I'll play either at the drop of a hat anywhere. But yes, I suppose my reputation, based upon some experiences I've had, is pretty much as advertised.' (I said something to the effect that I'd certainly seen no sign of it; very much the opposite, in fact. Another snort:) 'Look, you're a writer, you're a director, you function behind the camera. You do not appear upon the

88

screen, forty feet high and thirty feet wide or whatever the proportions are. Me, I'm an actress, and I do appear upon that screen, that big. What I say and do, and how I look, is what millions of people see and listen to. The fact that my performance is the end result of many other contributions as well, matters to them not at all. If I make a horse's ass of myself on that screen, it is I — me — Bette Davis — who is the forty-feet-by-thirty-feet horse's ass as far as they're concerned. Not the writer, not the director, the producer or the studio gateman — nobody but me. I am up there as the representative horse's ass for all concerned.

" 'Now you know as well as I' (she went on) 'that there is nothing more important to an actress, nothing she wants more, than a well-written part — and a director who knows what he wants, knows how to ask for it, who can help her provide it. *This* is heaven, for instance.' (She said some nice things about my script, and about how well we worked together.) '*But*, as often as not, the script has been at best a compromise of some sort; the writer's guarantee ran out, or the producer's patience, or just plain time. So, you've turned to the director as the source of salvation; with his help, you think, it'll turn out fine. Or, at least, hold together.

" 'Then, one morning, the director drops by your dressing room, casual-like, for a cup of coffee — and in a very strange voice asks what you think of the scene you're about to do that day, and do you really like it. That *does* it, for me. Right now. When you've been through it as often as I have, that does it. Bells and sirens go off inside me. I know at once that *he* doesn't like the scene — that *he* doesn't know what to think about it. Invariably, rehearsal proves me right. The director can't make up his mind whether we're to stand, sit, run, enter, or exit; he hasn't the foggiest notion of what the scene is all about or whether, in fact, it's a scene at all. He may suddenly bawl the hell out of some member of the crew for no reason — just to *do* something. The producer's been sent for — God knows where the writer is by now — and the producer's assistant — maybe an executive or two — and pretty soon there's quite a gathering of overhead on the set, throwing worn-out clichés at each other.

" 'By this time, I am back in my stage dressing room. Fully aware — as you would be, as any of the many, many actors who have gone through that time after time would be — that the result of it all, nine times out of ten, will be a botched-up abortive scene which will wind up with me as a thirty-by-forty-foot horse's ass on the silver screen. So. It seems I made up my mind, a long time ago, that if anybody is to make a horse's ass out of me, it's going to be *me*. So, yes, I'm afraid there have been times — and probably will be again — when the responsibility for what I say and do on the screen is one I feel I must meet by myself.'

"I haven't phrased Bette's position nearly as well as she told it to me. I've made it sound too much like just another bit of *Once in a Lifetime* foolery; it wasn't, really. It was a vivid and precise statement of the two sources of support upon which the good actor must rely, and without which he cannot fully function. First of all, that part. Soundly constructed, and so properly phrased that the actor can absorb the 'alias' comfortably and confidently. And number two, the director. The leader, if you will, of the theatrical conspiracy (and I'll defend that as properly defining either a play or film). The director is not only 'in' on all the 'aliases' (or parts — and there is no word in theatrical terminology which should be more literally interpreted); he must control their interplay and interrelation, from the broadest sweep of action to the least perceptible nuance of mood; his is the responsibility for the eventual coalescence of all the separate parts into the one dramatic whole. So — the sound script, the equipped actor, the prepared director — the three basic components of the theatrical conspiracy. Only rarely will it successfully overcome the weakest of the three.

"There were, of course, actors (make that Stars) who were indulged in childishly excessive demands that in no way improved the quality of their work; they served merely to sustain whatever offstage ego-fantasies they were enjoying at the time. Overelaborate dressing-room suites, stereo equipment on the set (complete with recordings to accompany their daydreamings, and a retainer — on the company payroll — who did nothing but change the discs), a stand-by limousine whose sole function was to take them to the toilet (I'm not kidding), and too many other infantile indulgences. The major studios started that nonsense, too. (It was, after all, cheaper to give so-and-so a black onyx bidet than a raise in salary. The bidet stayed on the lot, as inventory. It was charged to capital improvement, not picture cost.)

"Nor have directors been innocent of such self-indulgent absurdities. C. B. DeMille *did* have His (with a capital H) 'chair boy' — a staff member who followed Him around, chair in hand, ready to shove it under His ass at the precise instant He chose to sit. There were directors, too, who had music especially piped in to accompany their cogitations. At one time, if you wanted to speak to Joe von Sternberg on his set, you wrote your name on a huge blackboard set up for that purpose — and waited for the Imperial Nod. Directors, by the dozen, wear 'uniforms' which can serve only to establish immediately for the visitor's eye just which one is the director. They sure as hell don't help him direct. There's that darling of the *Cahiers du Cinema* who starts — or used to start — every scene by firing a .45 caliber revolver; there's the yeller-louder-than-anybody-else type; there's the coat-over-the-shoulders school — one wonders how Fellini manages to get his work done in an ordinary pair of pants, white shirt, jacket, and sometimes even a necktie.

"I have found, though, in my own experience, that zany behavior while at work (and I stress 'at work' can be equated, usually, in inverse ratio to the talent at hand. (Ask a precocious child to spell a word or do a sum she should be able to but can't — i.e., own up to even temporary inadequacy — and watch her act the clown as a reactive cover-up.) Bette Davis' discourse was not applicable to such. Nor to those actors and directors who 'play' big-time actor and who 'play' big-shot director for self-assurances of whatever nature. Bette had reference to the serious artist of indisputable talent, whose demands on the set were in the cause of optimum working conditions, but who was nevertheless bruited about as being 'difficult.' Quite a different cup of tea from the limousine-to-the-toilet brew. I know whereof I speak. I've drunk a-plenty from both cups.

"A word or two might be in order here on behalf of the so-called 'difficult' actor. As a theatrical epithet, it's applied much too readily — and much too often as an easy cop-out for shoddy dramatic material and/or irresolute direction. I've worked, as I say, with many of the most notoriously 'difficult.' Not always without sizable script weaknesses to overcome; nor, as director, have I always been omnisciently ready with that exactly right answer to the problem at hand. But with one Notable Exception — after more than forty years of writing, directing, and producing for and with actors, with some of whom it's been pretty rough going, indeed — there isn't one whose behavior I can honestly describe as having been motivated by any purpose other than giving the best damn performance possible. And with whom, at the end of our engagement, I didn't wind up on the best of terms. 'Engagement.' The word has the connotation of love, an emotion not necessarily involved in the theatrical experience.

"The Notable Exception? No, it was not Marlon Brando. Not even close. But he's a good example of what I mean by the too-easy application of the epithet 'difficult.' I've worked twice with Brando. Each venture was something new for both of us. I'd never directed Shakespeare professionally; Marlon had never played it at all. You may recall the snickering reaction when it was announced that he was to play Mark Antony; to the TV and other comics of the day, that bit of casting was a richer source of material than Spiro Agnew as Vice-President of the United States. We worked hard and long together, just the two of us; he worked his ass off, preparing by himself. After the film was released, the jokes stopped. The British Film Academy (Shakespeare, remember, is all that's left of the Empire) gave Marlon its award for best performance by a foreign actor (Gielgud's Cassius was judged best by an Englishman). We had every right to be happy about our collaboration on *Julius Caesar*, and we were. I can't recall a moment of 'difficulty' from Marlon; there was neither time nor occasion for it, we were both too occupied with working hard at something we wanted to do well.

"The same was true even of *Guys and Dolls*. Here again we were trying a dramatic style and form strange to both of us: musical comedy. I had staged an opera for the Met;*

* In 1952 Mankiewicz directed Puccini's *La Bohème* for the Metropolitan Opera. His original staging, altered according to the whims

93

dubious preparation for a stylized fairy tale set in Damon Runyon's Never-Never Land. Marlon, as far as I knew, had never sung or danced. Actually, he turned down the role of Sky Masterson when Sam Goldwyn first offered it to him. I was in Europe at the time, finishing up *The Barefoot Contessa*; Sam phoned and asked me to intercede. I sent Marlon a cable: UNDERSTAND YOU'RE APPREHENSIVE BECAUSE YOU'VE NEVER DONE MUSICAL COMEDY. YOU HAVE NOTHING REPEAT NOTHING TO WORRY ABOUT. BECAUSE NEITHER HAVE I. LOVE, JOE. Marlon promptly signed to do the part.

"Whether or not we succeeded in carrying it off to everybody's satisfaction — the differences of opinion were varied and vehement — is beside the point I'm talking to at the moment. The point being Marlon Brando, the 'difficult' actor. There was no more evidence of it on *Guys and Dolls* than there had been on *Julius Caesar*; we worked together equally hard and well on both films. Directing Marlon was an exciting and rewarding experience at all times; I found him quick, sensitive, and of course enormously talented. Naturally, if I'd ask him to do or think or feel something contrary to his instincts or intuition, we'd have to work that out. But, hell, that, too, is what directing is about. And acting.

"The Notable Exception, surprisingly enough, wasn't any of the male actors I've directed. Yes, that narrows it down by half. No, it was not Elizabeth Taylor. Talk about bum raps. I think I'm as knowledgeable about Elizabeth — or was throughout the time of the Great Brouhaha — as any of the

---

of changing prima donnas over the years, was eventually billed, at his request, as Mankiewicz' "production of." The most successful production of *La Bohème* in the history of the "Met," it was the last regular opera presented when the old "Met" closed on April 16, 1966.

94

Public Scolds who were, and remain, in pursuit of her like a pack of self-righteous beagles after a strangely unwily vixen. Believe me, I have been privy, and sometimes closer, to much of the offscreen, offstage delinquency of theatre-folk; it is indistinguishable in every way from that of the extended-lunch-hour, 'just shopping, dear . . .' private people. Except, perhaps, for the attractiveness of the participants.

"There's more of it, to be sure, among theatre-folk; their behavior, after all, is motivated more by emotion than calculation. But among those theatre-folk, Elizabeth Taylor is one of the least promiscuous, one of the least profligate beautiful women I have ever known. Perhaps if she had been more calculating and conniving — techniques more palatable to the morality mores she's reputed to have outraged — she'd have saved a great deal of wear and tear on herself. But she took it. Head on. It's the only way she knew; hardly that of a schemer. Elizabeth is a good and generous and honest human being. I'm her friend.

"As an actress, I thought she might have become a brilliant one. And still might. For a while, her personal tribulations seemed to have become interwoven with her work; how could they not have? When all at once her public image ceased being that of an actress — and became, instead, a sitting-duck target with unlimited free shots for all comers? We worked together twice; I'm quite sure Elizabeth recalls the second with no more joy than I do — although she wound up with a more valued memento than I did.

"But *Suddenly, Last Summer* was in every way a gratifying experience for both of us. It wasn't my screenplay; it was by Tennessee Williams and Gore Vidal. Their locutions were characteristically elaborate and stylized, not easy to commit to memory and demanding a great variety of approach in the playing. The last-act 'aria' of the girl, Catherine (Elizabeth), was as long and difficult a speech, I venture, as any ever attempted on the screen. It was also the dramatic climax of the film. There was no compromise possible: either it came off, or you could drop everything that had gone before into the out-take bin.

"Well, after four or five takes I called a break; we'd been close, but no cigar. Maybe a short rest would do it. Then somebody, one of the gaffers I think, waved at me — and took me around behind the set. There, slumped on the floor beside a flat, was Elizabeth. Physically and emotionally exhausted. Sobbing in great dry gulps. Convinced she'd let herself and everybody else down. This was no 'showboat' for the benefit of agent, lover/husband, or just attention-getting; I'd seen too many of those, by masters of malingering, to be taken in. Elizabeth had quite simply been brought to her knees by her own demands upon herself. Her talent is primitive in its best meaning: she hadn't the techniques for rationing herself; her emotional commitment was total each time.

"So I squatted beside her and made a very calculated suggestion, knowing damned well what the reaction would be. I proposed wrapping it for that day — and starting again, fresh, in the morning. I got the answer I expected. 'Tomorrow, my ass' (in effect), said Elizabeth, 'I'll do it now.' She got up, fixed her make-up, Jack Hildyard hit the lights — and the next take was the print. Elizabeth's performance in *Suddenly, Last Summer*, particularly that last, long Williams 'aria,' was quite remarkable, I think. Run it again some time, and study it — objectively. If that's presently possible about anything Elizabeth does, or did.

"Of course, it might not reflect the aesthetic implications of Antonioni's wall — and it might not reveal those tran-

96

scendental nuances with which entranced cinema buffs endow the stoic stare of almost any continental actress through a rain-swept windshield — surely the film directors of the Common Market countries can do no less than establish a memorial to the inventor of the windshield wiper — but you'll rarely come across a more honestly realized performance by an actress.

"No, the least of my problems have been with so-called 'difficult' good actors and actresses. The Notable Exception? I've told you she was female, and very Notable — and we've eliminated the most obvious guess. No, not Ava Gardner, either. She was a joy. No more guesses. I never talk about, or identify, Notable Exceptions."

V

Mankiewicz delivered his rough cut of *All About Eve* by the end of June; the next two months were given over to final editing and scoring. It was during this time that the film was shorn of the footage which clearly established and maintained the three interrelated points of view which formed the narrative structure and — in particular — the replaying of Eve's scene about the meaning of applause as first Margo and then Karen recall it. Mankiewicz strongly opposed the deletion. (Although he prefers not to discuss his creative tanglings with Zanuck, it seemed obvious to me that the eliminations still rankled.)

At any rate, when the time approached for the scoring of the film, Mankiewicz apparently thought it politic to present his thoughts about the music in the form of a lengthy detailed memo to both Darryl Zanuck and Alfred Newman, who had been assigned to compose the score. Essentially he stressed the importance of having the music thematically identify each of the narrators and their subject, Eve. The entire memorandum reflects clearly Mankiewicz' concern about retaining, as far as possible, the original interwoven structure of his film. Near the beginning of it, he writes:

"Three characters tell the story of Eve: Addison, Karen, and Margo. In other words, the musical entity of our film consists of a basic theme, *Eve* — and three very different variations on that theme, coloured by the three very distinct characterizations of Addison, Karen, and Margo. These, of course, are supportive to the basic *Eve* theme — to which we give full play particularly at the film's end when Eve, too, is fully revealed and when the audience sees her not through any one else's eyes but her own." Again, in the last paragraph of his memorandum:

"The very finish would be the *Eve* theme — out in the open for the first time. Emphasizing the emptiness and bitterness of what she is. The final music cue should start after the last line of dialogue in the film. It should build constantly, underscoring and underlining the cumulative steps by which the little girl from Brooklyn (Phoebe) assumes Eve's character — first her mantle, then her manner — indicating clearly that she will become another Eve — and finally the full realization, dramatically and musically, that the world is filled with Eves and that they will be with us always. (The mirror SHOT)."

All About Eve had its premiere at the Roxy Theatre in New York on October 13, 1950. Critically, it received unanimously glowing reviews from all eight (at the time) daily newspapers. As the release of the film widened, accompanied by the enthusiastic word-of-mouth endorsement of its audiences, so did the flow of critical acclaim.

(There were a few exceptions, most notable for their scarcity. *Life* magazine dismissed the film as an inept attempt to denigrate aging actresses. Leo Rosten in *Look*, on the other hand, acclaimed it as "by all odds, the most literate film of the year" and as "an incisive piece of anthropology — a field trip into that curious and specialized society known as the Theatre" while asserting that "Mankiewicz has put the seal of personal monopoly on an entire area of dramatic material — the field of social commentary.")

Abroad, the reception of *All About Eve*, was, if anything, even more enthusiastic — and the negative appraisals even fewer. The English critics, ever chary with superlatives, were unstinting in their approval; their glowing reviews were prophetic of its ultimate designation by the British Film Academy "as the best film from any source released in Great Britain during the year 1950." Dubbed into as many foreign languages as the countries of its world-wide release, the film continued to gather critical acclaim and awards — ranging from First Prize at the Cannes Film Festival (of which, oddly, Mankiewicz has never received any official notification) to "Best Picture" citations and trophies from sources so geographically far-flung as Cuba and Japan.

(Commenting on the fact that more often than not, his work has been reviewed more thoughtfully and appreciatively abroad than here in America, Mankiewicz observed drily: "My films — particularly those I write as well as direct — seem to lose something in the original English.")

Even had he been so inclined, Mankiewicz could not have enumerated for me all of the awards accumulated by *All About Eve*. Unhappily, in 1951, while he was in the process of abandoning Los Angeles as his habitat to become once more a resident of New York, one of the moving vans carrying his effects crashed and was consumed by fire en route. As a result almost all of his files, manuscripts, correspondence, and professional mementos dating back to 1929 were destroyed. It was a tragic, irreplaceable loss for Mankiewicz — and obviously for film historians as well. Understandably enough, as he puts it:

"Forgive me, but I can't attach much importance to the fact that somewhere in those melted filing cabinets was the dust of a few more back-patting certificates or statuettes. I don't mean to sound ungrateful. It's just that I miss so terribly all of my project notebooks, my manuscripts, my letters and diaries — the private documentation of my twenty-year stretch out there."

Whatever the intrinsic merits or significance of awards may be, qualitative or quantitative, *All About Eve* must surely be the most honored screenplay ever written. In addition to the host of scrolls and citations from regional literary and/or film groups, and "Book and Author" societies, there were widely publicized medallions and trophies from *Look*, *Holiday*, the Foreign Correspondents Association, and other organizations. It was chosen Best of the Year by both the Writers Guild of America (screenplay) and the Directors Guild of America (direction). *All About Eve* was also the first individual screenplay to have been published in hardbound format. Much in demand over the years by aficionados of the screenplay, copies of the original printing (Random House, 1951) — when available in secondhand bookshops — now sell for upwards of twenty-five dollars.

At the twenty-third annual award ceremonies of the Academy of Motion Picture Arts and Sciences, in March 1951, *All About Eve* established two records which more than twenty years later have yet to be equaled. For one, Mankiewicz, by winning two Oscars — one for screenplay and another for direction — became the first, and remains thus far the only, film maker to have been awarded four Oscars in two consecutive years for both writing and directing. (In 1950 he had won the same two Oscars for *A Letter to Three Wives*: one for his screenplay, and one for his direction.) The other record was set by the film itself. *All About Eve* received no less than fourteen nominations for Academy Awards, a figure which has also not yet been equaled.

Unfortunately affecting the number of ultimate Oscar winners — but nevertheless clearly indicating the high regard by the Academy members for their accomplishments — all four of the leading actresses were nominated. Bette Davis and Anne Baxter received two of the five nominations for "Best Actress"; Thelma Ritter and Celeste Holm were two of the five nominated for "Best Supporting Actress." Miss Baxter and Miss Davis were therefore competing for the "Eve vote," as were Miss Ritter and Miss Holm in their category.

The outcome was foreseeable, and not uncommon when two or more candidates from the same film are among the five nominees: the split in the voting resulted in none of the four winning the coveted Oscar. George Sanders, however, the lone male nominee of the cast, was awarded an Oscar as "Best Supporting Actor." Additional Oscars were won for best costume design and best sound recording. *All About Eve* was chosen "Best Picture of the Year." Darryl Zanuck, accepting the award as its producer, simply held up his Oscar and said, "Thank you, Joe."

Earlier that year, on January 28, it had been the intention of the New York Film Critics to present their annual awards from the stage of the Radio City Music Hall. However, 1951 was also the year of Cardinal Spellman's public condemnation, as blasphemous, of *The Miracle,* which had been chosen (as part of the trilogy, *Ways of Love*) Best Foreign-Language Film.* Mounting threats of picketing and a Roman Catholic boycott against the Music Hall necessitated withdrawing the ceremonies to the Rainbow Room of the RCA building where they were held privately, entrance "by invitation" only. As Mankiewicz described it: "The first public award, I should think, ever to be presented furtively."

The New York Film Critics had chosen *All About Eve* for the "Best English Language Film" of 1950, Bette Davis for "Best Performance," and Mankiewicz for "Best Director." Darryl Zanuck was not in attendance; Spyros Skouras appeared on his behalf. Both Miss Davis and Mankiewicz were very much present. (As if corroborating Mankiewicz' earlier reminiscences to me about the Davis–Bankhead identification crisis, *The New York Times,* in reporting the occasion, wrote: "Speculation concerning the real-life identity of the stage star portrayed by Miss Davis had been lively, with the name of Tallulah Bankhead mentioned most frequently. In his receptance remarks, Mr. Mankiewicz sought to settle the matter by saying:

'It might be fitting here to disclose that the woman who was in my thoughts, who always has fascinated me, was none other than Peg Woffington of the old Drury Lane.'

"Both the Old Drury Lane Theatre," continued *The Times,* "and Miss Woffington have been dead for at least a century.")

* Joseph Burstyn, the distributor of the film, who had fought for and won the landmark decision against the hitherto unchallenged censorship power of the New York Catholic Diocese, was to receive the citation on behalf of the film's three directors: Pagnol, Renoir, and Rosselini.

Bette Davis, after receiving her citation, said of Mankiewicz (again, as reported by *The Times*): "We all followed
him blindly, and this is Joe's night." It was Leonard Lyons,
however, in the *New York Post*, who recounted the particular
actress–director exchange in the course of the ceremony
which has since become an oft-repeated theatrical anecdote.
As Lyons reported it:

"When Bette Davis received her Film Critics Circle prize
for *All About Eve*, she paid glowing tribute to Joe Mankiewicz, insisting that he alone was responsible for her performance; he'd written her lines, directed her every move
and inflection, etc. Then she pulled Mankiewicz — who had
already accepted his own award — to the platform for another bow. 'Bette forgot to tell you,' said Mankiewicz, 'that
on the seventh day I rested.' "

Twenty years later, almost to the day — on January 19,
1971 — Miss Davis and Mankiewicz were once more on hand,
at the invitation of the New York Film Critics, this time to
present the "Best Actress" and "Best Director" awards for the
year (Glenda Jackson for *Women in Love*; Robert Rafelson
for *Five Easy Pieces*). From the ovation which greeted Miss
Davis — and in particular, the appreciative response to an
abundance of "inside" quips which presupposed an intimate
knowledge of the film's content* — it was evident that the
film, and her performance in it, had not only emerged during
the intervening two decades as film classics, but that her

---

* Among the so-called cult films, *All About Eve* has long been one of
the all-time favorites. As in Mart Crowley's play, *The Boys in the Band*,
the true *Eve* cultist will have committed to memory large segments
of Mankiewicz' screenplay.

103

personal identification with it had become so marked as to suggest that *All About Eve* might more fittingly have been entitled *"All About Margo."*

Indeed, the part of the actress is written with such unrelenting larger-than-life bravura and is so enhanced by the memorable *tour de force* of Miss Davis that it becomes difficult to accept the role of Margo as nevertheless a supportive one within the structure of Mankiewicz' screenplay. As he pointed out more than once (even stressed in his memorandum concerning the scoring), Margo is but one of three narrators of an entity which is, after all, all about Eve. One recalls almost with disbelief the fact that Margo (and thus Bette Davis) appears practically not at all in the last third of the film.

This dramaturgical reality apparently either escaped the attention of, or was ignored by, the talents who converted *All About Eve* into a Broadway musical comedy entitled *Applause* (March 1970). It was designed as essentially a vehicle for the actress playing Margo (Lauren Bacall). Therefore, the roles of Eve and Karen being reduced to virtual nonentities (and that of Addison DeWitt incomprehensibly eliminated, his plot functions fused to a witless version of the producer Max Fabian), the librettists were inevitably faced with the dilemma of having no second act. As a result, their only recourse was to have Margo, after Bill walks out on her, repeat endlessly her need for him in both song and dialogue (drained of Mankiewicz' wit) until enough time has elapsed for the final curtain.

(At Mankiewicz' request, I must point out that any appraisal of *Applause* contained herein is my own. The musical version of *All About Eve* was another topic he preferred not to discuss, especially qualitatively, except to make it crystal clear that he was in no way involved with the production —

and that he has received no compensation of any kind for the utilization of his screenplay and direction. However, some of what he had to say is illuminative, I think, of major studio control over creative talent, particularly at the time *All About Eve* was made.)

"I wrote and directed *All About Eve*," said Mankiewicz, "as a salaried employee, a 'gun for hire,' as it were. As studio contracts were then written, whether you were Bill Faulkner, Bob Sherwood, Joe Blow, or Joe Mankiewicz, every conceivable right to what you created — in every conceivable medium, past, present, or yet to be invented (my Paramount writing contracts as far back as 1932 refer by name to the television rights!) — was, in every conceivable aspect, turned over to the studio. As if the studio were, in fact, the creator. Apparently, under the laws of equity, a craftsman who is paid to create a specific article for a specific medium — i.e., a photoplay to be projected upon a screen in a movie theatre — can be utterly deprived of any future relation to, or compensation for, his creation, even if it is utilized in a quite different medium for a quite different purpose. I know of no instance in which such incredible contractual usurpations have even been challenged.

"Twentieth Century-Fox, for instance, in regard to *All About Eve*, I assume, receives an 'author's' royalty from the *Applause* production. If so, it has by now undoubtedly taken in infinitely more than it paid me for writing and directing the film. Fox was also, I've been told, legally within its rights to permit the stage producers, adaptors and director to utilize my writing and direction — and to append their names as authors of what I had created. Fox, I'm told, was not even obligated to notify me of the contemplated production. Nor, in fact, did it do so.

"No, the legality of the position of all concerned with

Applause is apparently unassailable. As to the morality of the position — professional or otherwise — I keep remembering Bill Fields once telling me (talking of his carnival and circus days) the true purpose of the sign on the box office which reads: 'No mistakes rectified after leaving the window.' It was to keep the short-changed rube from yelling 'copper.' "

VI

What, I asked Mankiewicz, would he regard, in retrospect, as personally the most gratifying aspect of *All About Eve*'s enduring high repute as a film? Could he point to any one particular accomplishment within the film — or tribute from without — which had afforded him the greatest amount of personal gratification? He grinned at the question, seemed to welcome it, and answered without hesitation:

"Whatever else *All About Eve* may have been, or is, or will be as a film — it has already provided for me, as a writer, a reward bestowed upon only the very few. Certainly very few such as I, within the craftsman category. Please note that I said reward, not award. Actually, it was a particular award that culminated in the reward — both uniquely attributable to *Eve*:

"Every good satirist — and I am, or have been, or have tried to be, a good one — directs the probe of his satire at what he believes to be a truth: a fact of manners or mores or morality which society either evades, disguises, or denies. And, thus probing, hopes to penetrate the sham and expose said truth or fact. The goal of every satirist would be to have his satiric point proved valid; his dream would be to have its validity established by the very object of his satire, itself. Just as there can be no greater gratification for the author than to have his fantasy become reality. To have nature, however restricted in scope, mirror his art — however small the *a*.

"As I told you, way back — somewhere in that mountain of cassettes — my original concept of *All About Eve* was, and remained, to tell a satiric tale of theatre-folk, utilizing the flashback techniques within a satirical framework of the presentation and acceptance of that theatrical totem known as The Award. Creating a physical setting for the ceremony was no problem: it became a vague amalgam of the New York Players Club, of which I had been a member for many years, and the Garrick Club in London. But dreaming up a name for the theatrical society itself was less easy; it had to serve, after all, also as the inspiration for the physical appearance of the award. Then one day while I was rummaging through some old theatrical portraits to choose some to be reproduced and used as set dressing — Sir Joshua Reynolds' famous portrait of Sarah Siddons as *The Tragic Muse* popped up at me. And that was it.

"So, sometime early in 1950, I created both 'The Sarah Siddons Society' and that award which is presented annually for 'Distinguished Achievement in the Theatre': 'The Sarah Siddons Award.' Working from an enlarged print of the Reynolds portrait, the Twentieth Century-Fox prop shop started making up statuettes according to my specifications. The first approved model of 'The Sarah Siddons Award' is right over there, on my mantelpiece. Walter Scott (the set dresser) even put my name on it. So actually I was the first recipient of the 'Sarah Siddons Award.' So much for the fictional materialization of my fantasy, in 1950.

"*All About Eve* had its widest general release throughout 1951. Then sometime early in 1952 — as far as I have been able to determine—those charged with such responsibilities at the Ambassador East Hotel in Chicago bethought themselves of an inspired publicity gimmick for their Pump Room Restaurant and its eighteenth-century English ambience. The inspiration, I have been informed, struck both James Hart and Ernest Byfield, Jr., of the Ambassador East's administration; whether or not it was a simultaneous revelation, I do not know.

"But, *mirabile dictu*, in 1952, in Chicago, a 'Sarah Siddons Society' came into being. It had as its avowed purpose the furthering and flowering of the Theatrical Arts in that meat-orientated metropolis — and established, as symbolic of its lofty undertaking, 'The Sarah Siddons Award.' It was to be bestowed annually upon an actress chosen by the society for 'Distinguished Achievement' in the Theatre of Chicago — a feat not easy of accomplishment out where the winds of culture blow cold. The presentation ceremony, one may assume, would be destined to become a traditional rite at the — surprise, surprise — Ambassador East Hotel. So much for reality plagiarizing my fantasy, in 1952.

"Could anyone conceivably have been taken in by such an 'Award'? With *All About Eve* and its satiric connotations about 'Awards' still playing the movie theatres of Chicago? With the ads, magazines, Sunday supplements, and lobby displays still filled with exploitation layouts for the film, always featuring the 'Sarah Siddons Award' which I had dreamed up as an object of satire? An award of which the Chicago gimmick version was, what's more, an *exact replica?* You can bet your ass it was taken seriously.

"And not only by those culture-hungry matrons of Chicago

108

who to this day attend meetings faithfully and deliberate the winner with all the solemnity of the Nobel Prize Committee. Their 'Award,' from its very inception, became a much-sought-after accolade by many of our most distinguished actresses. It has endured for twenty years now, this bit of my intended satiric fantasy which has become unintended satiric reality. Yes, I'm quite prepared to accept your estimate that, next to the Tony Award, the 'Sarah Siddons Award' is the most treasured trophy for an actress in the American Theatre.

"Its first recipient, in 1953, was none other than Helen Hayes. Since then, among others similarly honored by this reproduction of my movie prop have been such actresses as: Beatrice Lillie, Deborah Kerr, Nancy Kelly, Geraldine Page, Shirley Booth, Gertrude Berg, Carol Channing — and of late, of all people, Celeste Holm. I can't help wondering whether Celeste had a feeling of *déjà vu*. Or whether she placed it alongside the 'Sarah Siddons Award' I gave her when we finished the film (the one her playwright-husband passed on to her). She probably threw out that old original fake. I hope she keeps the new fake fake. I wish long life both to the 'Sarah Siddons Society' and to its 'Award,' believe me. They will provide for me an annual and infinitely gratifying reaffirmation of what *All About Eve* was really all about."

As he envisaged all those Sarah Siddons Awards multiplying into infinity, a gleam came into Mankiewicz' eyes. He seemed to be recalling the film's final prismatic image: that in which Eves and Awards and the hunger for applause are projected endlessly into the future. With as much chagrin as relish, Mankiewicz added a final word on the subject:

"It would seem that the idiocies of theatre-folk within their world share with the idiocies of the outsiders, 'the private people,' within their world, one common characteristic. They are continuing, self-perpetuating idiocies."

All About Eve

a screenplay by
Joseph L. Mankiewicz

based on a short story by
Mary Orr

PRODUCED BY	Darryl F. Zanuck
WRITTEN FOR THE SCREEN AND DIRECTED BY	Joseph L. Mankiewicz
MUSIC	Alfred Newman
DIRECTOR OF PHOTOGRAPHY	Milton Krasner, ASC
ART DIRECTION	Lyle Wheeler, George W. Davis
SET DECORATIONS	Thomas Little, Walter M. Scott
FILM EDITOR	Barbara McLean
WARDROBE DIRECTION	Charles Le Maire
COSTUMES FOR MISS BETTE DAVIS	Designed by Edith Head
ORCHESTRATION	Edward Powell
MAKEUP ARTIST	Ben Nye
SPECIAL PHOTOGRAPHIC EFFECTS	Fred Sersen
SOUND	W. D. Flick, Roger Heman

CAST

MARGO CHANNING	Bette Davis
EVE HARRINGTON	Anne Baxter
ADDISON DE WITT	George Sanders
KAREN RICHARDS	Celeste Holm
BILL SAMPSON	Gary Merrill
LLOYD RICHARDS	Hugh Marlowe
BIRDIE	Thelma Ritter
MISS CASWELL	Marilyn Monroe
MAX·FABIAN	Gregory Ratoff
PHOEBE	Barbara Bates
AGED ACTOR	Walter Hampden

All About Eve was first presented by Twentieth Century-Fox Film Corporation at the Roxy Theatre, New York City, on October 13, 1950.

FADE IN

DINING HALL — SARAH SIDDONS SOCIETY — NIGHT

It is not a large room and jammed with tables; mostly for four but some for six and eight. A long table of honor, for about thirty people, has been placed upon a dais.

Dinner is over. Demi-tasses, cigars and brandy. The over-all effect is one of worn elegance and dogged gentility. It is June.

The CAMERA, as it has been throughout the CREDIT TITLES, is on a

FULL CLOSEUP

of the SARAH SIDDONS AWARD. It is a gold statuette, about a foot high, of Sarah Siddons as "The Tragic Muse." Exquisitely framed in a nest of flowers, it rests on a miniature altar in the center of the table of honor.

OVER THIS we hear the crisp, cultured, precise VOICE of ADDISON DE WITT:

> ADDISON'S VOICE
> *The Sarah Siddons Award for Distinguished*

115

Achievement is perhaps unknown to you. It has been spared the sensational and commercial publicity that attends such questionable "honors" as the Nobel Prize — and those awards presented annually by that film society . . .

The CAMERA has EASED BACK to include some of the table of honor and a distinguished gentleman with snow-white hair who is speaking. He is a few years either side of 100. We do not hear what he says.

ADDISON'S VOICE

The distinguished-looking gentleman is an extremely old actor. Being an actor, he will go on speaking for some time. It is not important that you hear what he says.

The CAMERA EASES BACK some more, and CONTINUES until it discloses a fairly COMPREHENSIVE SHOT of the room.

ADDISON'S VOICE

However, it is important that you know where you are, and why you are here. This is the dining hall of the Sarah Siddons Society. The occasion is its annual banquet and presentation of the highest honor our Theatre knows — the Sarah Siddons Award for Distinguished Achievement.

116

A GROUP OF WAITERS

Clustered near the screens masking the entrances to the kitchen. The screens are papered with old theatrical programs. The waiters are all aged and venerable. They look respectfully toward the speaker . . .

ADDISON'S VOICE

These hallowed walls, indeed many of these faces, have looked upon Modjeska, Ada Rehan and Minnie Fiske. Mansfield's voice filled this room. Booth breathed this air. It is unlikely that the windows have been opened since his death.

CLOSE — THE AWARD

On its altar, it shines proudly above five or six smaller altars which surround it and which are now empty.

ADDISON'S VOICE

The minor awards, as you can see, have already been presented. Minor awards are for such as the writer and director — since their function is merely to construct a tower so that the world can applaud a light which flashes on top of it . . .

(the CAMERA MOVES to an EXTREME CLOSEUP of the Award)

. . . and no brighter light has ever dazzled the eye than Eve Harrington. Eve. But more of Eve, later. All about Eve, in fact . . .

CLOSE — ADDISON DEWITT

Not young, not unattractive, a fastidious dresser, sharp
of eye and merciless of tongue. An omnipresent cigarette
holder projects from his mouth like the sword of
D'Artagnan.

He sits back in his chair, musingly, his fingers making
little cannonballs out of bread crumbs. His narration
covers the MOVE of the CAMERA to him:

> ADDISON'S VOICE
> To those of you who do not read, attend the
> theatre, listen to unsponsored radio programs or
> know anything of the world in which you live — it
> is perhaps necessary to introduce myself.
>   (CAMERA IS ON him now)
> My name is Addison DeWitt. My native habitat
> is the Theatre — in it I toil not, neither do I spin.
> I am a critic and commentator. I am essential to
> the Theatre — as ants to a picnic, as the boll
> weevil to a cotton field . . .

He looks to his left. The CAMERA MOVES to a

CLOSEUP — KAREN RICHARDS

She is lovely and thirtyish in an unprofessional way. She
is scraping bread crumbs, spilled sugar, etc., into a little

118

pile with a spoon. Addison takes one of her bread crumbs. She smiles absently . . .

CLOSEUP — ADDISON

He rolls the bread crumb into a cannonball.

> ADDISON'S VOICE
> *This is Karen Richards. She is the wife of a playwright, therefore of the Theatre by marriage. Nothing in her background or breeding should have brought her any closer to the stage than row E, center . . .*

CLOSEUP — KAREN

She continues her doodling.

> ADDISON'S VOICE
> *. . . however, during her senior year at Radcliffe, Lloyd Richards lectured on the drama. The following year Karen became Mrs. Lloyd Richards. Lloyd is the author of Footsteps on the Ceiling, the play which has won for Eve Harrington the Sarah Siddons Award . . .*

Karen absently pats the top of her little pile of refuse. A hand reaches in to take the spoon away. Karen looks as the CAMERA PANS with IT to a

CLOSEUP — MAX FABIAN

He sits at her left. He's a sad-faced man with glasses and a look of constant apprehension. He smiles apologetically and indicates a white powder which he unwraps. He pantomimes that his ulcer is snapping.

CLOSE — KAREN

She smiles back, returns to her doodling.

CLOSE — ADDISON

He mashes a cigarette stub, pops it out of his holder. He eyes Max.

> ADDISON'S VOICE
>
> *There are in general two types of theatrical producers. One has a great many wealthy friends who will risk a tax-deductible loss. This type is interested in Art.*

CLOSE — MAX

He drops the powder into some water, stirs it, drinks, burps delicately and closes his eyes.

> ADDISON'S VOICE
>
> *The other is one to whom each production means potential ruin or fortune. This type is out to make a buck. Meet Max Fabian. He is the producer of*

*the play which has won for Eve Harrington the
Sarah Siddons Award . . .*

Max rests fitfully. He twitches. A hand reaches into the
SCENE, removes a bottle of Scotch from before him. The
CAMERA follows the bottle to a

CLOSEUP — MARGO CHANNING

She sits at Max's left, at DeWitt's right. An attractive,
strong face. She is childish, adult, reasonable, unreason-
able — usually one when she should be the other, but
always positive. She pours a stiff drink.

CLOSE — ADDISON

He holds out the soda bottle to her.

CLOSE — MARGO

She looks at it, and at him, as if it were a tarantula and
he had gone mad.

CLOSE — ADDISON

He smiles and pours a glass of soda for himself.

ADDISON'S VOICE

*Margo Channing is a Star of the Theatre. She
made her first stage appearance, at the age of four,
in Midsummer Night's Dream. She played a fairy*

and entered — quite unexpectedly — stark naked. She has been a Star ever since.

CLOSE — MARGO

She sloshes her drink around moodily, pulls at it.

> ADDISON'S VOICE
> Margo is a great Star. A true Star. She never was or will be anything less or anything else . . .
> (slight pause)
> . . . the part for which Eve Harrington is receiving the Sarah Siddons Award was intended originally for Margo Channing.

CLOSE — ADDISON

Having sipped his soda water, he puts a new cigarette in his holder, leans back, lights it, looks and exhales in the general direction of the table of honor.

As he speaks the CAMERA MOVES in the direction of his glance . . .

> ADDISON'S VOICE
> *Having covered in tedious detail not only the history of the Sarah Siddons Society, but also the history of acting since Thespis first stepped out of the chorus line — our distinguished chairman has finally arrived at our reason for being here . . .*

At this point Addison's voice FADES OUT and the voice of
the aged actor FADES IN. CAMERA is in a MEDIUM CLOSE
SHOT of him and the podium.

> AGED ACTOR
>
> I have been proud and privileged to have spent my
> life in the Theatre — "a poor player . . . that
> struts and frets his hour upon the stage" — and I
> have been honored to be, for forty years, Chief
> Prompter of the Sarah Siddons Society . . .

THE SARAH SIDDONS AWARD

As the aged actor's hands lift it from its altar.

> AGED ACTOR'S VOICE
>
> Thirty-nine times have I placed in deserving hands
> this highest honor the Theatre knows . . .

AGED ACTOR

He grows a bit arch, he uses his eyebrows.

> AGED ACTOR
>
> Surely no actor is older than I. I have earned my
> place out of the sun . . .
>
> (indulgent laughter)
>
> . . . and never before has this Award gone to any-
> one younger than its recipient tonight. How fitting
> that it should pass from my hands to hers . . .

EVE'S HANDS

Lovely, beautifully groomed. In serene repose, they rest between a demi-tasse and an exquisite small evening bag.

AGED ACTOR'S VOICE
Such young hands. Such a young lady. Young in years, but whose heart is as old as the Theatre . . .

ADDISON

His eyes narrow quizzically as he listens. Then, slowly, he turns to look at Karen . . .

AGED ACTOR'S VOICE
Some of us are privileged to know her. We have seen beyond the beauty and artistry —

KAREN

She never ceases her thoughtful pat-a-cake with the crumbs.

AGED ACTOR'S VOICE
— that have made her name resound through the nation. We know her humility. Her devotion, her loyalty to her art.

ADDISON

His glance moves from Karen to Margo.

AGED ACTOR'S VOICE

Her love, her deep and abiding love for us —

MARGO

Her face is a mask. She looks down at the drink which she
cradles with both hands.

AGED ACTOR'S VOICE

— for what we are and what we do. The Theatre.
She has had one wish, one prayer, one dream. To
belong to us.

AGED ACTOR

He's nearing his curtain line.

AGED ACTOR

Tonight her dream has come true. And henceforth
we shall dream the same of her.
            (a slight pause)
Honored members, ladies and gentlemen — for
distinguished achievement in the Theatre — the
Sarah Siddons Award to Miss Eve Harrington!

FULL SHOT

The entire room is galvanized into sudden and tumultuous applause. Some of the more enthusiastic gentlemen
rise to their feet. Flash bulbs start popping about halfway

125

down the table to the Aged Actor's left . . . EVE starts
to rise —

CLOSE — EVE

She rises into it and the CAMERA MOVES CLOSER. Eve.
Beautiful, radiant, poised, exquisitely gowned. She stands
in simple and dignified response to the ovation.

HER ANGLE

A dozen photographers skip, squat and dart about like
water bugs. Flash bulbs pop and pop and pop . . .

THE WAITERS

They applaud enthusiastically . . .

AGED ACTOR

Award in hand, he beams at her . . .

EVE

She smiles sweetly to her left, then to her right . . .

MAX

He's come to. He applauds lustily.

ADDISON

Applauding too — more discreetly.

126

MARGO

Not applauding. But you sense no deliberate slight, merely an impression that as she looks at Eve her mind is on something else . . .

KAREN

Nor is she applauding. But her gaze is similarly fixed on Eve in a strange, faraway fashion . . .

ADDISON

Still applauding, his eyes flash first at Margo and then at Karen. Then he directs them back to Eve. He smiles ever so slightly . . .

EVE

The applause has continued unabated. She turns now, and moves gracefully toward the Aged Actor, the CAMERA MOVING with her. She moves through applauding ladies and gentlemen; from below the flash bulbs keep popping . . .

As she nears her goal, the Aged Actor turns to her. He holds out the award. Her hand reaches out for it. At that PRECISE MOMENT — with the award JUST BEYOND HER FINGERTIPS — THE PICTURE HOLDS, THE ACTION STOPS. The SOUND STOPS. ADDISON'S VOICE takes over:

Eve. Eve, the Golden Girl. The cover girl, the girl next door, the girl on the moon. . . . Time has been good to Eve. Life goes where she goes — she's been profiled, covered, revealed, reported, what she eats and when and where, what she wears and when and where, whom she knows and where she was and when and where she's going. . . .

CLOSEUP — ADDISON

He's stopped applauding, he's sitting forward, staring intently at Eve . . . his narration continues unbroken.

ADDISON'S VOICE

. . . Eve. You all know all about Eve. . . . what can there be to know that you don't know . . . ?

As he leans back, the APPLAUSE FADES IN as tumultuous as before. Addison's look moves slowly from Eve to Karen.

CLOSEUP — KAREN

She leans forward now, her eyes intent on Eve. Her lovely face FILLS THE SCREEN as the APPLAUSE FADES ONCE MORE — as she thinks back:

KAREN'S VOICE

When was it? How long? It seems a lifetime ago. Lloyd always said that in the Theatre a lifetime was

128

*a season, and a season a lifetime. It's June now.
That was — early October . . . only last October.
It was a drizzly night, I remember I asked the taxi
to wait . . .*

Her last lines are over a —

SLOW DISSOLVE TO:

NEW YORK THEATRE STREET — NIGHT

Traffic is not heavy; the shows have broken some half-hour
before. The rain is just a drizzle.

There are other theatres on the street; display lights are
being extinguished. Going out just as Karen's taxi pulls
up is: MARGO CHANNING in AGED IN WOOD.

CLOSER

As the taxi comes to a stop at the alley. Karen can be seen
through the closed windows telling the driver to wait.
Then she gets out. She takes a step, hesitates, then looks
about curiously:

> KAREN'S VOICE
> *Where was she? Strange . . . I had become so
> accustomed to seeing her there night after night —
> I found myself looking for a girl I'd never spoken
> to, wondering where she was . . .*

She smiles a little at her own romanticism, puts her head down and makes her way into the alley.

ALLEY — NIGHT

CAMERA MOVING with Karen toward the stage door. She passes a recess in the theatre wall — perhaps an exit — about halfway.

>   EVE'S VOICE
>   (softly)
>   Mrs. Richards . . .

Karen hesitates, looks. Eve is barely distinguishable in the shadow of the recess. Karen smiles, waits. Eve comes out. A gooseneck light above them reveals her . . .

She wears a cheap trench coat, low-heeled shoes, a rain hat stuck on the back of her head . . . her large, luminous eyes seem to glow up at Karen in the strange half-light.

>   KAREN
>   So there you are. It seemed odd, suddenly, your
>   not being there . . .

>   EVE
>   Why should you think I wouldn't be?

>   KAREN
>   Why should you be? After all, six nights a week —
>   for weeks — of watching even Margo Channing
>   enter and leave a theatre —

130

EVE

I hope you don't mind my speaking to you . . .

KAREN

Not at all.

EVE

I've seen you so often — it took every bit of courage I could raise —

KAREN
(smiles)
To speak to just a playwright's wife? I'm the lowest form of celebrity.

EVE

You're Margo Channing's best friend. You and your husband are always with her — and Mr. Sampson . . . what's he like?

KAREN
(grins)
Bill Sampson? He's — he's a director.

EVE

He's the best.

KAREN

He'll agree with you. Tell me — what do you do between the time Margo goes in and comes out? Just huddle in that doorway and wait?

                              EVE

Oh, no. I see the play.

                             KAREN
                         (incredulous)
You see the play? You've seen the play every
performance?
                       (Eve nods)
But, don't you find it — I mean apart from everything else — don't you find it expensive?

                              EVE

Standing room doesn't cost much. I manage.

Karen contemplates Eve. Then she takes her arm.

                             KAREN

I'm going to take you to Margo . . .

                              EVE
                        (hanging back)
Oh, no . . .

                             KAREN

She's got to meet you —

                              EVE

No, I'd be imposing on her, I'd be just another
tongue-tied gushing fan . . .

Karen practically propels her toward the stage door.

KAREN

(insisting)

There isn't another like you, there couldn't be —

EVE

But if I'd known . . . maybe some other time . . .
I mean, looking like this . . .

KAREN

You look just fine . . .
(they're at the stage door)
. . . by the way. What's your name?

EVE

Eve. Eve Harrington.

Karen opens the door. They go in.

BACKSTAGE — NIGHT

Everything, including the doorman, looks fireproof.

Eve enters like a novitiate's first visit to the Vatican.
Karen, with a "Good evening, Gus —" to the doorman,
leads the way toward Margo's stage dressing room. Eve,
drinking in the wonderment of all she surveys, lags
behind. Karen waits for her to catch up . . .

EVE

You can breathe it — can't you? Like some magic
perfume . . .

133

Karen smiles, takes Eve's arm. They proceed to Margo's dressing room.

OUTSIDE MARGO'S DRESSING ROOM

No star on the closed door; the paint is peeling. A typewritten chit, thumbtacked, says MISS CHANNING.

As Karen and Eve approach it, an uninhibited guffaw from Margo makes them pause.

> KAREN
> (whispers)
> You wait a minute . . .
> (she smiles)
> . . . now don't run away —

Eve smiles shakily. At the same moment:

> MARGO'S VOICE
> (loudly — through the door)
> "Honey chile," I said, "if the South had won the war, you could write the same plays about the North!"

Karen enters during the line.

MARGO'S DRESSING ROOM — NIGHT

It is a medium-sized box, lined with hot-water pipes and

cracked plaster. It is furnished in beat-up wicker. A door leads to an old-fashioned bathroom.

Margo is at the dressing table. She wears an old wrapper, her hair drawn back tightly to fit under the wig which lies before her like a dead poodle. Also before her is an almost finished drink.

LLOYD RICHARDS is stretched out on the wicker chaise. He's in his late thirties, sensitive, literate.

Between them, by the dressing table, is BIRDIE — Margo's maid. Her age is unimportant. She was conceived during a split week in Walla Walla and born in a carnival riot. She is fiercely loyal to Margo.

Karen enters during the line Margo started while she was outside. Lloyd chuckles, Birdie cackles.

KAREN	MARGO
Hi.	Hi.
(she goes to kiss Lloyd)	(she goes right on —
Hello, darling —	in a thick "Suth'n" ac-
	cent)
LLOYD	"Well, now, Mis' Chan-
How was the concert?	nin', ah don't think you
	can rightly say we lost
KAREN	the wah, we was mo'
Loud.	

BIRDIE

Lemme fix you a drink.

KAREN

No, thanks, Birdie.

stahved out, you might say — an' that's what ah don' unnerstand about all these plays about sex-stahved Suth'n women — sex is one thing we was nevah stahved for in the South!"

Karen laughs with them.

LLOYD

Margo's interview with a lady reporter from the South —

BIRDIE

The minute it gets printed they're gonna fire on Gettysburg all over again . . .

MARGO

It was Fort Sumter they fired on —

BIRDIE

I never played Fort Sumter.

She takes the wig into the bathroom. Margo starts creaming the makeup off her face.

MARGO

Honey chile had a point. You know, I can remem-

136

ber plays about women — even from the South —
where it never even occurred to them whether
they wanted to marry their fathers more than their
brothers . . .

That was way back . . .

MARGO

Within your time, buster. Lloyd, honey, be a
playwright with guts. Write me one about a nice,
normal woman who shoots her husband.

Birdie comes out of the bathroom without the wig.

BIRDIE

You need new girdles.

MARGO

Buy some.

BIRDIE

The same size?

MARGO

Of course!

BIRDIE

Well. I guess a real tight girdle helps when you're
playin' a lunatic.

137

She picks up Lloyd's empty glass, asks "more?" He shakes his head. She pours herself a quick one.

KAREN

(firmly)
Margo does not play a lunatic, Birdie.

BIRDIE

I know. She just keeps hearin' her dead father play a banjo.

MARGO

It's the tight girdle that does it.

KAREN

I find these wisecracks increasingly less funny! *Aged in Wood* happens to be a fine and distinguished play —

LLOYD

— 'at's my loyal little woman.

KAREN

The critics thought so, the audiences certainly think so — packed houses, tickets four months in advance — I can't see that either of Lloyd's last two plays have hurt you any!

LLOYD

Easy, now . . .

MARGO

(grins)

Relax, kid. It's only me and my big mouth . . .

KAREN

(mollified)

It's just that you get me so mad sometimes . . .
of all the women in the world with nothing to
complain about —

MARGO

(dryly)

Ain't it the truth?

KAREN

Yes, it is! You're talented, famous, wealthy — people waiting around night after night just to see
you, even in the wind and rain . . .

MARGO

Autograph fiends! They're not people — those little beasts who run in packs like coyotes —

KAREN

They're your fans, your audience —

MARGO

They're nobody's fans! They're juvenile delinquents, mental defectives, they're nobody's audi-

ence, they never see a play or a movie, even —
they're never indoors long enough!

There is a pause. Lloyd applauds lightly.

> KAREN
>
> Well . . . there's one indoors now. I've brought
> her back to see you.

> MARGO
>
> You've *what?*

> KAREN
>
> (in a whisper)
> She's just outside the door.

> MARGO
>
> (to Birdie — also a whisper)
> The heave-ho.

Birdie starts. Karen stops her. It's all in whispers, now,
until Eve comes in.

> KAREN
>
> You can't put her out, I promised . . . Margo,
> you've got to see her, she worships you, it's like
> something out of a book —

> LLOYD
>
> That book is out of print, Karen, those days are
> gone. Fans no longer pull the carriage through

the streets — they tear off clothes and steal wrist
watches . . .

                        KAREN
If you'd only see her, you're her whole life — you
must have spotted her by now, she's always
there . . .

                        MARGO
Kind of mousy trench coat and funny hat?
                    (Karen nods)
How could I miss her? Every night and matinee —
well . . .

Karen goes to the door, opens it. Eve comes in. Karen
closes the door behind her. A moment.

                        EVE
          (simply)
I thought you'd forgotten about me.

                        KAREN
Not at all.
              (her arm through Eve's)
Margo, this is Eve Harrington.

Margo changes swiftly into a first-lady-of-the-theatre
manner.

MARGO

(musically)

How do you do, my dear?

BIRDIE

(mutters)

Oh, brother.

EVE

Hello, Miss Channing.

KAREN

My husband . . .

LLOYD

(nicely)

Hello, Miss Harrington.

EVE

How do you do, Mr. Richards?

MARGO

(graciously)

And this is my good friend and companion, Miss
Birdie Coonan.

BIRDIE

Oh, brother.

EVE

Miss Coonan . . .

142

LLOYD
(to Birdie)
Oh, brother what?

BIRDIE
When she gets like this . . . all of a sudden she's
playin' Hamlet's mother.

MARGO
(quiet menace)
I'm sure you must have things to do in the bathroom, Birdie dear.

BIRDIE
If I haven't, I'll find something till you're normal.

She goes into the bathroom.

MARGO
Dear Birdie. Won't you sit down, Miss Worth-
ington?

KAREN
Harrington.

MARGO
I'm so sorry . . . Harrington. Won't you sit down?

EVE
Thank you.

She sits. A short lull.

MARGO	KAREN
Would you like a drink?	I was telling Margo and
It's right beside you . . .	Lloyd about how often
	you'd seen the play . . .

They start together, and stop in deference to each other.
They're a little flustered. But not Eve.

EVE

(to Margo)

No, thank you.

(to Lloyd)

Yes. I've seen every performance.

LLOYD

(delighted)

Every performance? Then — am I safe in assuming
you like it?

EVE

I'd like anything Miss Channing played . . .

MARGO

(beams)

Would you, really? How sweet —

LLOYD

(flatly)

I doubt very much that you'd like her in *The
Hairy Ape.*

144

EVE

Please don't misunderstand me, Mr. Richards. I think that part of Miss Channing's greatness lies in her ability to choose the best plays —

MARGO

(sighs)

And there's so little to choose from these days . . .

KAREN

(warningly)

Margo . . .

LLOYD

And then there's always the playwright's problem — whom can we borrow from Hollywood to play it?

MARGO

(icily)

I understand that Hopalong Cassidy is looking for something.

EVE

(deftly averting the squall)

Your new play is for Miss Channing, isn't it, Mr. Richards?

MARGO

Of course it is.

LLOYD

How'd you hear about it?

EVE

There was an item in the *Times*. I like the title.
Footsteps on the Ceiling.

LLOYD

Let's get back to this one. Have you really seen
every performance?

(Eve nods)
Why? I'm curious.

Eve looks at Margo, then drops her eyes.

EVE

Well. If I didn't come to see the play, I wouldn't
have anywhere else to go.

MARGO

There are other plays . . .

EVE

Not with you in them. Not by Mr. Richards . . .

LLOYD

But you must have friends, a family, a home —

Eve pauses. Then shakes her head.

146

KAREN

Tell us about it — Eve.

Eve looks at her — grateful because Karen called her "Eve." Then away, again . . .

EVE

If I only knew how . . .

KAREN

Try . . .

EVE

Well . . .

Birdie comes out of the bathroom. Everybody looks at her sharply. She realizes she's in on something important. She closes the door quietly, leans against it.

EVE

Well . . . it started with the play before this one.

LLOYD

Remembrance.

EVE

(nods)
Remembrance.

MARGO

Did you see it here in New York?

San Francisco. It was the last week. I went one
night . . . the most important night of my life —
until this one. Anyway . . . I found myself going
the next night — and the next and the next. Every
performance. Then, when the show went East —
I went East.

BIRDIE

I'll never forget that blizzard the night we played
Cheyenne. A cold night. First time I ever saw a
brassiere break like a piece of matzo.

Eve looks up at her unsmilingly, then back to her hands.

KAREN

Eve . . . why don't you start at the beginning?

EVE

It couldn't possibly interest you.

MARGO

Please . . .

Eve speaks simply and without self-pity:

EVE

I guess it started back home. Wisconsin, that is.
There was just Mum and Dad — and me. I was
the only child, and I made believe a lot when I
was a kid — I acted out all sorts of things . . .

148

what they were isn't important. But somehow acting and make-believe began to fill up my life more and more. It got so that I couldn't tell the real from the unreal except that the unreal seemed more real to me . . . I'm talking a lot of gibberish, aren't I?

LLOYD

Not at all . . .

EVE

Farmers were poor in those days, that's what Dad was — a farmer. I had to help out. So I quit school and I went to Milwaukee. I became a secretary. In a brewery.

(she smiles)

When you're a secretary in a brewery — it's pretty hard to make believe you're anything else. Everything is beer. It wasn't much fun, but it helped at home — and there was a Little Theatre group . . . like a drop of rain on a desert. That's where I met Eddie. He was a radio technician. We played *Liliom* for three performances, I was awful — then the war came, and we got married. Eddie was in the Air Force — and they sent him to the South Pacific. You were with the O.W.I., weren't you, Mr. Richards?

(Lloyd nods)

That's what *Who's Who* says . . . well, with Eddie gone, my life went back to beer. Except for a letter a week. One week Eddie wrote he had a leave coming up. I'd saved my money and vacation time. I went to San Francisco to meet him.

(a slight pause)

Eddie wasn't there. They forwarded the telegram from Milwaukee — the one that came from Washington to say that Eddie wasn't coming at all. That Eddie was dead . . .

(Karen puts her hand on Lloyd's)

. . . so I figured I'd stay in San Francisco. I was alone, but I couldn't go back without Eddie. I found a job. And his insurance helped . . . and there were theatres in San Francisco. And one night Margo Channing came to play in *Remembrance* . . . and I went to see it. And — well — here I am . . .

She finishes dry-eyed and self-composed. Margo squeezes the bridge of her nose, dabs at her eyes.

BIRDIE

(finally)

What a story! Everything but the bloodhounds snappin' at her rear end.

That breaks the spell. Margo turns on her —

MARGO

There are some human experiences, Birdie, that do not take place in a vaudeville house — and that even a fifth-rate vaudevillian should understand and respect!

(to Eve)

I want to apologize for Birdie's —

BIRDIE

(snaps in)

You don't have to apologize for me!

(to Eve)

I'm sorry if I hurt your feelings. It's just my way of talkin' . . .

EVE

(nicely)

You didn't hurt my feelings, Miss Coonan.

BIRDIE

Call me Birdie.

(to Margo)

As for bein' fifth rate — I closed the first half for eleven years an' you know it!

She slams into the bathroom again. At that precise instant BILL SAMPSON flings open the door to the dressing room. He's youngish, vital, undisciplined. He lugs a beat-up suitcase which he drops as he crosses to Margo —

151

BILL

Forty-seven minutes from now my plane takes off and how do I find you? Not ready yet, looking like a junk yard —

MARGO

Thank you so much.

BILL

Is it sabotage, does my career mean nothing to you? Have you no human consideration?

MARGO

Show me a human and I might have!

KAREN

(conscious of Eve)

Bill . . .

BILL

The airlines have clocks, even if you haven't! I start shooting a week from Monday — Zanuck is impatient, he wants me, he needs me!

KAREN

(louder)

Bill —

MARGO

Zanuck, Zanuck, Zanuck! What are you two — lovers?

Bill grins suddenly, drops to one knee beside her.

> BILL
>
> Only in some ways. You're prettier . . .

> MARGO
>
> I'm a junk yard.

> KAREN
>
> > (yells)
>
> Bill!

> BILL
>
> > (vaguely — to Karen)
>
> Huh?

> KAREN
>
> This is Eve Harrington.

Bill flashes a fleeting look at Eve.

> BILL
>
> Hi.
>
> > (to Margo)
>
> My wonderful junk yard. The mystery and dreams
> you find in a junk yard —

> MARGO
>
> > (kisses him)
>
> I love a psychotic.

Bill grins, rises, sees Eve as if for the first time.

BILL

Hello, what's your name?

EVE

Eve. Eve Harrington.

KAREN

You've already met.

BILL

Where?

KAREN

Right here. A minute ago.

BILL

That's nice.

MARGO

She, too, is a great admirer of yours.

BIRDIE

Imagine. All this admiration in just one room.

BILL

You. Take your mistress into the bathroom and
dress her.
(Birdie opens her mouth)
Without comment.

Birdie shuts it and goes into the bathroom. In a moment
we hear a shower start to run. Eve gets up.

154

KAREN

You're not going, are you?

EVE

I think I'd better. It's been — well, I can hardly find the words to say how it's been . . .

MARGO

(rises)
No, don't go . . .

EVE

The four of you must have so much to say to each other — with Mr. Sampson leaving . . .

Margo, impulsively, crosses to Eve.

MARGO

Stick around. Please. Tell you what — we'll put Stanislavsky on his plane, you and I, then go somewhere and talk.

EVE

Well — if I'm not in the way . . .

MARGO

I won't be a minute.

She darts into the bathroom. Eve sits down again.

KAREN

Lloyd, we've *got* to go —

Lloyd gets up. Karen crosses to pound on the bathroom door. She yells — the shower is going . . .

KAREN

Margo, good night! I'll call you tomorrow!

Margo's answer is lost in the shower noise. Karen crosses to kiss Bill. She's joined by Lloyd.

KAREN

Good luck, genius . . .

BILL

Geniuses don't need good luck.
(he grins)
I do.

LLOYD

I'm not worried about you.

BILL

Keep the thought.

They shake hands warmly. Karen and Lloyd move to Eve.

KAREN

Good night, Eve. I hope I see you again, soon —

EVE

I'll be at the old stand, tomorrow matinee —

KAREN

Not just that way. As a friend.

156

EVE

I'd like that.

LLOYD

It's been a real pleasure, Eve.

EVE

I hope so, Mr. Richards. Good night.

Lloyd shakes her hand, crosses to join Karen who waits at the open dressing-room door.

EVE

Mrs. Richards . . .
            (Karen and Lloyd look back)
I'll never forget this night as long as I live. And I'll never forget you for making it possible . . .

Karen smiles warmly. She closes the door. They leave.

BACKSTAGE

CAMERA PANS Karen and Lloyd as they cross toward the stage door.

KAREN'S VOICE

— and I'll never forget you, Eve. Where were we going that night, Lloyd and I? Funny, the things you remember — and the things you don't . . .

MARGO'S DRESSING ROOM — NIGHT

Eve sits on the same chair. Bill keeps moving around. Eve
never takes her eyes off him. He offers her a cigarette.
She shakes her head. He looks at his watch.

> EVE
>
> You said forty-seven minutes. You'll never make it.

> BILL
>
> (grins)
>
> I told a lie. We'll make it easily. Margo's got no
> more conception of time than a halibut.

He sprawls on the chaise, closes his eyes. A pause.

> EVE
>
> (finally)
>
> So you're going to Hollywood.

Bill grunts in the affirmative. Silence.

> BILL
>
> Why?

> EVE
>
> I just wondered.

> BILL
>
> Just wondered what?

> EVE
>
> Why.

158

BILL

Why what?

EVE

Why you have to go out there.

BILL

I don't have to. I want to.

EVE

Is it the money?

BILL

Eighty per cent of it will go for taxes.

EVE

Then why? Why, if you're the best and most successful young director in the theatre —

BILL

The Theatuh, the Theatuh —
          (he sits up)
— what book of rules says the Theatre exists only
within some ugly buildings crowded into one
square mile of New York City? Or London, Paris
or Vienna?
          (he gets up)
Listen, junior. And learn. Want to know what the
Theatre is? A flea circus. Also opera. Also rodeos,

carnivals, ballets, Indian tribal dances, Punch and Judy, a one-man band — all Theatre. Wherever there's magic and make-believe and an audience — there's Theatre. Donald Duck, Ibsen and The Lone Ranger. Sarah Bernhardt, Poodles Hanneford, Lunt and Fontanne, Betty Grable — Rex the Wild Horse and Eleanora Duse. You don't understand them all, you don't like them all — why should you? The Theatre's for everybody — you included, but not exclusively — so don't approve or disapprove. It may not be your Theatre, but it's Theatre for somebody, somewhere . . .

EVE

I just asked a simple question.

BILL

(grins)
And I shot my mouth off. Nothing personal, junior, no offense . . .
(he sits back down)
. . . it's just that there's so much bushwah in this Ivory Green Room they call the Theatuh — sometimes it gets up around my chin . . .

He lies down again.

EVE

But Hollywood. You mustn't stay there.

160

BILL

(he closes his eyes)
It's only a one-picture deal.

EVE

So few come back . . .

BILL

Yeah. They keep you under drugs out there with
armed guards . . .

A pause.

EVE

I read George Jean Nathan every week.

BILL

Also Addison DeWitt.

EVE

Every day.

BILL

You didn't have to tell me.

Margo, putting on an earring, buzzes out of the bathroom
followed by Birdie. Bill sits up.

MARGO

(en route)
I understand it's the latest thing — just one ear-

ring. If it isn't, it's going to be — I can't find the other . . .

She grabs her pocketbook, starts rummaging. Out comes a letter.

BILL

Throw that dreary thing away, it bores me —

Margo drops it in the wastebasket, keeps rummaging.

EVE

(concerned)
Where do you suppose it could be?

BIRDIE

It'll show up.

MARGO

(gives up)
Oh, well . . .
(to Birdie)
. . . look through the wigs, maybe it got caught —

BILL

Real diamonds in a wig. The world we live in.

MARGO

(she's been looking)
Where's my coat?

BIRDIE

Right where you left it . . .

She goes behind the chaise. She comes up with a magnificent mink.

BILL

(to Margo)
The seams.

Margo starts to straighten them.

MARGO

(to Eve)
Can't keep his eyes off my legs.

BILL

Like a nylon lemon peel —

MARGO

(straightens up)
Byron couldn't have said it more graciously. Here we go —

By now she's in the coat and has Eve's arm, heading for the door. Bill puts his arms around Birdie.

BILL

Got any messages? What do you want me to tell Tyrone Power?

BIRDIE

Just give him my phone number. I'll tell him myself.

Bill kisses her cheek. She kisses Bill.

BIRDIE

Kill the people.
(to Margo)
Got your key?

MARGO

(nods)
See you home . . .

Margo and Eve precede Bill out of the door.

DISSOLVE TO:

LA GUARDIA FIELD — NIGHT

Baggage counter. The rain has stopped, but it's wet.

Margo, Eve and Bill are stymied behind two or three couples waiting to be checked in. Margo's arm is through Bill's. They become increasingly aware of their imminent separation. Eve senses her superfluity.

A lull. Bill cranes at the passenger heading the line, in earnest conversation with the dispatcher. He sighs.

164

MARGO

They have to time it so everybody gets on at the
last minute. So they can close the doors and let
you sit.

The man up ahead moves on.

BILL

Ah . . .

EVE

I have a suggestion.
          (they look at her)
There's really not much time left — I mean, you
haven't had a minute alone yet, and — well, I
could take care of everything here and meet you at
the gate with the ticket . . . if you'd like.

BILL

I think we'd like very much. Sure you won't mind?

EVE

Of course not.

Bill hands Eve the ticket. Margo smiles gratefully at her.
Eve smiles back.

PASSAGE AND GATE — LA GUARDIA — NIGHT

It's covered, with glass windows. CAMERA TRUCKS BEFORE
Margo and Bill. Her arm in his.

BILL

She's quite a girl, this what's-her-name . . .

MARGO

Eve. I'd forgotten they grew that way . . .

BILL

That lack of pretense, that sort of strange direct-
ness and understanding —

MARGO

Did she tell you about the Theatre and what it
meant?

BILL

(grins)
I told her. I sounded off.

MARGO

All the religions in the world rolled into one, and
we're gods and goddesses . . . isn't it silly, suddenly I've developed a big, protective feeling for
her — a lamb loose in our big stone jungle.

Bill pulls her to one side. Some passengers go by . . . the
CAMERA MOVES IN. A pause.

MARGO

Take care of yourself out there.

BILL

I understand they've got the Indians pretty well
in hand.

MARGO

Bill . . .

BILL

Huh?

MARGO

Don't get stuck on some glamour puss —

BILL

I'll try.

MARGO

You're not such a bargain, you know, conceited
and thoughtless and messy —

BILL

Everybody can't be Gregory Peck.

MARGO

You're a setup for some gorgeous wide-eyed young
babe.

BILL

How childish are you going to get before you quit
it?

167

I don't want to be childish, I'd settle for just a few
years —

BILL

(firmly)
And cut that out right now.

MARGO

Am I going to lose you, Bill? Am I?

BILL

As of this moment you're six years old . . .

He starts to kiss her, stops when he becomes aware of
Eve standing near them. She has his ticket in her hand.

EVE

All ready.

She hands Bill his ticket, they start toward the gate.

BOARDING GATE — LA GUARDIA — NIGHT

A few visitors. Bill hands his ticket to the guard, turns to
Eve.

BILL

Thanks for your help . . . good luck.

EVE

Good-bye, Mr. Sampson.

Bill puts his arms around Margo.

168

BILL

Knit me a muffler.

MARGO

Call me when you get in . . .

They kiss. Margo's arms tighten desperately. Bill pulls away, kisses her again lightly, starts for the plane. Margo turns away. Eve puts her arm through Margo's.

Bill pauses en route to the plane.

BILL

Hey — junior . . .

Margo turns to look at him with Eve.

BILL

Keep your eye on her. Don't let her get lonely. She's a loose lamb in a jungle . . .

Eve looks at Margo. Margo smiles.

EVE

Don't worry . . .

Bill waves, climbs aboard. The door is closed behind him, the departure routine starts.

Margo and Eve turn to go. They walk away from CAMERA down the PASSAGE. As they walk, Eve gently disengages her arm from Margo's and puts it comfortingly about her.

That same night we sent for Eve's things, her few pitiful possessions . . . she moved into the little guest room on the top floor . . . she cried when she saw it — it was so like her little room back home in Wisconsin.

The next three weeks were out of a fairy tale — and I was Cinderella in the last act. Eve became my sister, lawyer, mother, friend, psychiatrist and cop — the honeymoon was on . . .

SLOW DISSOLVE TO:

MARGO'S LIVING ROOM — DAY

It's one floor above street level. A long narrow room, smartly furnished — including a Sarah Siddons Award.

MARGO'S NARRATIVE continues over this scene which is a SILENT ONE.

Eve sits at a smart desk. She is just arranging a stack of letters which she carries to Margo with a pen. Margo sits comfortably by the fire with a play script. She hands the script up to Eve, shakes her head and holds her nose. Eve smiles, takes the script, hands Margo the letters to sign.

Birdie comes in with a tea tray which she sets on a low table before the fire.

170

The phone rings.

Birdie and Eve both go for it. Eve gets there first. By her polite but negative attitude, we know she is giving someone a skillful brush-off.

Birdie glares first at her, then at Margo.

Margo leans her head back, closes her eyes blissfully . . .

Birdie slams the double door to the landing on her way out.

DISSOLVE TO:

THEATRE — BACKSTAGE

From the wings. The audience is NEVER VISIBLE. Eve in the foreground, her back to CAMERA. Margo and company taking a curtain call. Tumultuous applause . . . the curtain falls. The cast, except for Margo and two male leads, walks off. The curtain rises again . . .

CLOSE — EVE

Watching and listening to the storm of applause. Her eyes shine, she clasps and unclasps her hands . . .

THE STAGE

Eve again in the foreground, but CLOSER. Again the curtain falls. This time the two men go off. Curtain rises on Margo alone. If anything, the applause builds . . .

CLOSEUP — EVE

That same hypnotic look . . . there are tears in her eyes.
The curtain falls offscene, then rises again —

CLOSE — MARGO

The curtain falls again between her and CAMERA . . .

BACKSTAGE

The curtain just settling on the floor. Margo starts off.

> STAGE MANAGER
>> One more?

> MARGO
>> (shakes her head)
>> From now on it's not applause — it's just some-
>> thing to do till the aisles get less crowded.

She walks as she talks and winds up at Eve — still in the
wings. Eve's eyes are wet, she dabs at her nose.

> MARGO
>> What — again?

> EVE
>> I could watch you play that last scene a thousand
>> times and cry every time —

> MARGO
>> (grins)
>> Performance number one thousand of this one —

if I play it that long — will take place in a well-padded booby hatch.

She takes Eve's arm, they stroll toward her dressing room.

                    EVE
I must say you can certainly tell Mr. Sampson's been gone a month.

                    MARGO
You certainly can. Especially if you're me between now and tomorrow morning.

                    EVE
I mean the performance. Except for you, you'd think he'd never even directed it — it's disgraceful the way they change everything around.

                    MARGO
        (smiles)
Well, teacher's away and actors will be actors.

                    EVE
During your second act scene with your father, Roger Ferraday's supposed to stay way upstage at the arch. He's been coming closer down every night.

                    MARGO
When he gets too close, I'll spit in his eye.

They're at her dressing room by now. Margo's been un-
hooking her gown, with Eve's help. They go in.

MARGO'S DRESSING ROOM — NIGHT

It's undergone quite a change. A new carpet, chintz
covers for the furniture, new lampshades, dainty curtains
across the filthy barred window.

Birdie waits within.

> MARGO
> (entering)
> You bought the new girdles a size smaller. I can
> feel it.

> BIRDIE
> Something maybe grew a size larger.

> MARGO
> When we get home you're going to get into one
> of those girdles and act for two and a half hours.

> BIRDIE
> I couldn't get into the girdle in two an' a half
> hours.

Margo's out of her wig and dress by now. She gets into
her robe, sits at the dressing table. Eve's on the chaise,
by the discarded costume.

174

EVE

You haven't noticed my latest bit of interior
decorating.

MARGO

(turns, looks)
Well, you've done so much . . . what's new?

EVE

The curtains. I made them myself.

MARGO

They are lovely. Aren't they lovely, Birdie?

BIRDIE

Adorable. We now got everything a dressing room
needs except a basketball hoop.

MARGO

Just because you can't even work a zipper. It was
very thoughtful, Eve, and I appreciate it —

A pause. Eve rises, picking up Margo's costume.

EVE

While you're cleaning up, I'll take this to the
wardrobe mistress —

MARGO

Don't bother. Mrs. Brown'll be along for it in a
minute.

EVE

No trouble at all.

And she goes out with the costume. Birdie opens her mouth, shuts it, then opens it again.

BIRDIE

If I may be so bold as to say something — did you ever hear the word "union"?

MARGO

Behind in your dues? How much?

BIRDIE

I haven't got a union. I'm slave labor.

MARGO

Well?

BIRDIE

But the wardrobe women have got one. And next to a tenor, a wardrobe woman is the touchiest thing in show business —

MARGO

(catching on)

Oh-oh.

BIRDIE

She's got two things to do — carry clothes an'

press 'em wrong — an' just let anybody else muscle in . . .

                              MARGO
                        (remembering)
Detroit.
                              (she jumps up)
Detroit! When you took that stain out — they nearly closed us . . .

She hurries to the door and out after Eve.

BACKSTAGE — OUTSIDE MARGO'S DRESSING ROOM

Margo pops out, looks for Eve, then stares in amazement:

EVE

Near the wings. She stands before a couple of cheval mirrors set up for cast members. She has Margo's dress held up against her body. She turns this way and that, bows as if to applause — mimicking Margo exactly.

MARGO

She watches her curiously. Then she smiles.

                              MARGO
                        (calling)
Eve —

EVE

Startled, she whips the gown away, turns to Margo . . .

MARGO

Smiles understandingly.

MARGO
(quietly)
I think we'd better let Mrs. Brown pick up the
wardrobe . . .

Wordlessly, Eve brings it toward her . . .

DISSOLVE TO:

MARGO'S BEDROOM — NIGHT

Margo's asleep. A bedside clock with a luminous dial
reads 3 A.M. exactly. The phone rings. Her head comes
up out of the pillow, she shakes it. She fumbles, switches
on a lamp, then picks up the phone.

MARGO
Hello . . .

OPERATOR'S VOICE
We are ready with your call to Beverly Hills . . .

MARGO
Call, what call?

OPERATOR'S VOICE

Is this Templeton 8-9970? Miss Margo Channing?

MARGO

That's right, but I don't understand —

OPERATOR'S VOICE

We are ready with the call you placed for 12 midnight, California time, to Mr. William Sampson in Beverly Hills . . .

MARGO

I placed . . . ?

OPERATOR'S VOICE

Go ahead, please . . .

BILL'S VOICE

(a loud, happy squawk)
Margo! What a wonderful surprise!

Margo jumps at his vehemence. BILL, when we reveal him during the scene, is also in bed. His clock says midnight.

BILL

(continuing)
What a thoughtful, ever-lovin' thing to do —

MARGO

(dazed)
Bill? Have I gone crazy, Bill?

BILL

You're my girl, aren't you?

MARGO

That I am . . .

BILL

Then you're crazy.

MARGO

(nods in agreement)

When — when are you coming back?

BILL

I leave in a week — the picture's all wrapped up, we previewed last night . . . those previews. Like opening out of town, but terrifying. There's nothing you can do, you're trapped, you're in a tin can —

MARGO

— in a tin can, cellophane or wrapped in a Navajo blanket, I want you home . . .

BILL

You in a hurry?

MARGO

A big hurry, be quick about it — so good night, darling, and sleep tight . . .

180

BILL

Wait a minute! You can't hang up, you haven't
even said it —

MARGO

Bill, you know how much I do — but over the
phone, now really, that's kid stuff . . .

BILL

Kid stuff or not, it doesn't happen every day, I
want to hear it — and if you won't say it, you can
sing it . . .

MARGO
(convinced she's gone mad)
Sing it?

BILL

Sure! Like the Western Union boys used to do . . .

Margo's eyes pop. Her jaw and the phone sag . . .

MARGO

Bill . . . Bill, it's your birthday.

BILL

And who remembered it? Who was there on the
dot, at twelve midnight . . . ?

Margo knows damn well it wasn't she.

181

MARGO

(miserably)

Happy birthday, darling . . .

BILL

The reading could have been better, but you said
it — now "many happy returns of the day . . ."

MARGO

(the same)

Many happy returns of the day . . .

BILL

I get a party, don't I?

MARGO

Of course, birthday and welcome home . . .
Who'll I ask?

BILL

(laughs)

It's no secret, I know all about the party — Eve
wrote me . . .

MARGO

She did . . . ?

BILL

She hasn't missed a week since I left — but you
know all that, you probably tell her what to write

182

. . . anyway, I sent her a list of people to ask —
check with her.

                    MARGO
Yeah . . . I will.

                    BILL
How is Eve? Okay?

                    MARGO
Okay.

                    BILL
I love you . . .

                    MARGO
          (mutters)
I'll check with Eve . . .

                    BILL
What?

                    MARGO
I love you, too. Good night, darling —

                    BILL
See you . . .

Margo hangs up. Bill hangs up. He replaces his phone,
picks up his book.

                                      183

Margo puts her phone away. She gets a cigarette. She lights it. She rolls over on her back . . .

DISSOLVE TO:

MARGO'S BEDROOM — DAY

Margo is propped up in bed, still reflective. Birdie comes in with her breakfast tray and a "Hi" which gets a "Hi" from Margo. She starts on some petty chores. Margo takes a sip of orange juice . . .

> MARGO

Birdie —

> BIRDIE

Hmm?

> MARGO

You don't like Eve, do you?

> BIRDIE

Do you want an argument or an answer?

> MARGO

An answer.

> BIRDIE

No.

> MARGO

Why not?

BIRDIE

Now you want an argument.

MARGO

She works hard.

BIRDIE

Night an' day.

MARGO

She's loyal and efficient —

BIRDIE

Like an agent with one client.

MARGO

She thinks only of me . . .
            (no answer from Birdie)
. . . doesn't she?

BIRDIE

            (finally)
Well . . . let's say she thinks only *about* you,
anyway . . .

MARGO

How do you mean that?

Birdie stops whatever it is she's doing.

BIRDIE

I'll tell you how. Like — let's see — like she was

studyin' you, like you were a play or a book or a
set of blueprints. How you walk, talk, think, eat,
sleep —

MARGO

(breaks in; sharply)

I'm sure that's very flattering, Birdie, and I'm
sure there's nothing wrong with it!

There's a sharp, brisk knock. Eve comes in. She's dressed
in a smart suit. She carries a leather portfolio.

EVE

Good morning!

Margo says "Good morning," Birdie says nothing. Eve
shows off the suit, proudly.

EVE

Well — what do you think of my elegant new
suit?

MARGO

Very becoming. It looks better on you than it did
on me.

EVE

(scoffs)

I can imagine. You know, all it needed was some
taking in here and letting out there — are you sure
you won't want it yourself?

MARGO

Quite sure. I find it just a bit too — too "Seven-teenish" for me . . .

EVE

(laughs)
Oh, come now, as though you were an old lady . . . I'm on my way. Is there anything more you've thought of — ?

MARGO

There's the script to go back to the Guild —

EVE

I've got it.

MARGO

— and those checks or whatever it is for the income-tax man.

EVE

Right here.

MARGO

It seems I can't think of a thing you haven't thought of . . .

EVE

(smiles)
That's my job.
            (she turns to go)
See you at tea time . . .

MARGO

Eve . . .

(Eve turns at the door)

. . . by any chance, did you place a call from me
to Bill for midnight California time?

EVE

(gasps)

Oh, golly. And I forgot to tell you —

MARGO

Yes, dear. You forgot all about it.

EVE

Well, I was sure you'd want to, of course, being
his birthday, and you've been so busy these past
few days, and last night I meant to tell you before
you went out with the Richards — and I guess I
was asleep when you got home . . .

MARGO

Yes, I guess you were. It — it was very thoughtful
of you, Eve.

EVE

Mr. Sampson's birthday. I certainly wouldn't forget that. You'd never forgive me.

(she smiles shyly)

As a matter of fact, I sent him a telegram myself . . .

188

And she's gone. Margo stares at the closed door. Then at Birdie. Birdie, without comment, goes out. Margo, alone, looks down at her orange juice. Absently, she twirls it in its bed of shaved ice . . .

SLOW DISSOLVE TO:

MARGO'S BEDROOM — NIGHT

It's January. The night of Margo's party for Bill. Margo is all dressed except for jewelry. She stands before her dressing table putting it on. She sips at an enormous Martini . . .

> MARGO'S VOICE
>
> *Bill's welcome-home-birthday party . . . a night to go down in history. Like the Chicago fire — or the Massacre of the Huguenots. Even before the party started, I could smell disaster in the air . . . I knew it, I sensed it even as I finished dressing for that blasted party . . .*

Birdie comes in.

> BIRDIE
>
> You all put together?

> MARGO
>
> My back's open.
> (Birdie goes to work on it)
> Did the extra help get here?

189

BIRDIE

There's some loose characters dressed like maids and butlers. Who'd you call — the William Morris Agency?

MARGO

You're not being funny. I could get actors for less. What about the food?

BIRDIE

The caterer had to go back for the hors d'oeuvres —
          (she zips Margo)
Voilà.

MARGO

          (laughs)
That French ventriloquist taught you a lot, didn't he?

BIRDIE

There was nothing he didn't know.
          (she starts tidying the room)
There's a message from the bartender. Does Miss Channing know she ordered domestic gin by mistake?

MARGO

The only thing I ordered by mistake is the guests.
          (Birdie cackles)
They're domestic, too, and they don't care what

they drink as long as it burns. Where's Bill? He's late.

BIRDIE

Late for what?

MARGO

Don't be dense. The party.

BIRDIE

I ain't dense. And he's been here twenty minutes.

MARGO

Well, I certainly think it's odd he hasn't even come up . . .

Her glance meets Birdie's. She turns and strolls out.

THIRD FLOOR LANDING — NIGHT

Margo speeds up going down the steps.

SECOND FLOOR LANDING — NIGHT

Margo slows up again deliberately as she reaches the landing. Sound of Bill and Eve laughing together from the living room. Margo strolls toward it casually as the CAMERA PANS with her.

We see Eve seated, looking up fascinatedly at Bill as he talks. Out of the laughter . . .

BILL

"Don't let it worry you," said the cameraman,

"Even DeMille couldn't see anything looking through the wrong end —"

(Eve chuckles)

So that was the first and last time —

Eve sees Margo approach. She gets up. Bill turns.

MARGO'S LIVING ROOM — NIGHT

As Margo strolls up, very off-hand.

> MARGO
> (casually)
> Don't let me kill the point. Or isn't it a story for grownups?

> BILL
> You've heard it. About when I looked through the wrong end of a camera finder.

> MARGO
> (to Eve)
> Remind me to tell you about when I looked into the heart of an artichoke.

> EVE
> I'd like to hear it.

> MARGO
> Some snowy night in front of the fire . . . in the meantime, while we're on the subject, will you

check about the hors d'oeuvres? The caterer forgot them, the paint wasn't dry or something . . .

EVE

Of course.

She leaves. A short lull. Margo looks into cigarette boxes.
Bill eyes her curiously, crosses to the fire.

BILL

Looks like I'm going to have a very fancy party . . .

MARGO

I thought you were going to be late —

BILL

When I'm guest of honor?

MARGO

I had no idea you were even here.

BILL

I ran into Eve on my way upstairs; she told me
you were dressing.

MARGO

That's never stopped you before.

BILL

Well, we started talking, she wanted to know all
about Hollywood, she seemed so interested . . .

193

MARGO

She's a girl of so many interests.

BILL

It's a pretty rare quality these days.

MARGO

She's a girl of so many rare qualities.

BILL

So she seems.

MARGO
(the steel begins to flash)

So you've pointed out, so often. So many qualities, so often. Her loyalty, efficiency, devotion, warmth, affection — and so young. So young and so fair . . .

Bill catches the drift. Incredulously.

BILL

I can't believe you're making this up — it sounds like something out of an old Clyde Fitch play . . .

MARGO

Clyde Fitch, though you may not think so, was well before my time!

BILL
(laughs)

I've always denied the legend that you were in

Our American Cousin, the night Lincoln was
shot . . .

MARGO

I don't think that's funny!

BILL

Of course it's funny — this is all too laughable to
be anything else. You know what I feel about this
— this age obsession of yours — and now this
ridiculous attempt to whip yourself up into a
jealous froth because I spent ten minutes with a
stage-struck kid —

MARGO

Twenty minutes!

BILL

Thirty minutes, forty minutes? What of it?

MARGO

Stage-struck kid . . . she's a young lady — of qualities. And I'll have you know I'm fed up with both
the young lady and her qualities! Studying me as
if — as if I were a play or a set of blueprints! How
I walk, talk, think, eat, sleep!

BILL

Now how can you take offense at a kid trying in
every way to be as much like her ideal as possible?

195

MARGO

Stop calling her a kid! It so happens there are particular aspects of my life to which I would like to maintain sole and exclusive rights and privileges!

BILL

For instance what?

MARGO

For instance — you!

BILL

This is my cue to take you in my arms and reassure you — but I'm not going to. I'm too mad —

MARGO

— guilty.

BILL

Mad! Darling, there are certain characteristics for which you are famous — on stage and off. I love you for some of them — and in spite of others. I haven't let those become too important to me. They're part of your equipment for getting along in what is laughingly called our environment — you've got to keep your teeth sharp. All right. But you will not sharpen them on me — or on Eve . . .

MARGO

What about her teeth? What about her fangs?

196

BILL

She hasn't cut them yet, and you know it! So when you start judging an idealistic dreamy-eyed *kid* by the barroom, benzedrine standards of this megalomaniac society — I won't have it! Eve Harrington has never by word, look, thought or suggestion indicated anything to me but her adoration for you and her happiness at our being in love! And to intimate anything else doesn't spell jealousy to me — it spells a paranoiac insecurity that you should be ashamed of!

MARGO

Cut! Print it! What happens in the next reel? Do I get dragged off screaming to the snake pit?

EVE'S VOICE
(quietly)
Miss Channing.

Bill and Margo look off. Eve is in the room. They have no way of knowing how long she's been there.

EVE

The hors d'oeuvres are here. Is there anything else I can do?

MARGO

Thank you, Eve. I'd like a Martini — very dry.

197

BILL

I'll get it.

(he crosses to Eve)

What'll you have?

Eve, involuntarily, looks to Margo.

MARGO

A milk shake?

Eve smiles, turns to Bill.

EVE

A Martini. Very dry, please.

Bill smiles back and starts across the landing toward the pantry. As he reaches the stairs, Karen, Lloyd and Max come up from the street level below. General greetings. Bill continues to the pantry. Eve and then Margo come up to add their welcome.

EVE

(to Karen)

May I have your coat?

KAREN

Don't bother, I can take it up myself . . .

EVE

Please.

Karen yields with a "Thank you, Eve." Eve goes up with the coat. Lloyd looks after her approvingly.

LLOYD

I like that girl. That quality of quiet gracious-
ness . . .

MARGO

. . . among so many quiet qualities.

They start for the living room.

KAREN

Margo, nothing you've ever done has made me
as happy as your taking Eve in . . .

MARGO

I'm so happy you're happy.

MAX

Look, you haven't been running a settlement
house exactly — the kid's earned her way. You had
a pretty mixed-up inventory when she took over —
merchandise laying all over the shop . . .

LLOYD

You've got Margo mixed up with a five-and-ten-
cent store . . .

MARGO

Make it Bergdorf Goodman . . . and now everything is on its proper shelf, eh, Max? Done up in
little ribbons. I could die right now and nobody'd
be confused. How about you, Max?

199

MAX

How about me what?

They've come to a halt near the fireplace.

MARGO

Suppose you dropped dead. What about your inventory?

MAX

I ain't gonna die. Not with a hit.

KAREN

This is the most ghoulish conversation . . .

Bill brings two Martinis. He hands one to Margo.

MARGO
(it drips ice)
Thank you.

BILL

Nothing, really.

MARGO

The kid — junior, that is — will be right down. Unless you'd like to take her drink up to her . . .

BILL
(smiles)
I can always get a fresh one. Karen — you're a Gibson girl . . .

He hands Eve's drink to Karen. Max has wandered off. Other guests are arriving. Margo gulps her drink, hands Bill the empty glass. He puts it on a passing tray. Margo takes a fresh one at the same time.

LLOYD

The general atmosphere is very Macbethish. What has or is about to happen?

MARGO

(to Bill)
What is he talking about?

BILL

Macbeth.

KAREN

(to Margo)
We know you, we've seen you before like this. Is it over — or just beginning?

Margo surveys them all.

MARGO

Fasten your seatbelts. It's going to be a bumpy night.

She downs the drink, hands the empty glass to Bill, and leaves them, CAMERA with her. She passes two women, gabbing by the piano. As they see her:

1ST WOMAN

Margo, darling!

2ND WOMAN

Darling!

MARGO

(passing)

Darlings . . .

She arrives at the landing just as Addison DeWitt comes up with MISS CASWELL. Miss Caswell is a blonde young lady, Addison's protégée-of-the-moment. Margo takes a drink from a passing tray.

MARGO

(to Addison)

I distinctly remember striking your name from the guest list. What are you doing here?

ADDISON

Dear Margo. You were an unforgettable Peter Pan — you must play it again, soon. You remember Miss Caswell?

MARGO

I do not. How do you do?

MISS CASWELL

We never met. Maybe that's why.

ADDISON

Miss Caswell is an actress. A graduate of the
Copacabana School of Dramatic Arts.
(his glance is attracted by Eve coming downstairs)
Ah . . . Eve.

EVE
(deferentially)
Good evening, Mr. DeWitt.

MARGO

I had no idea you knew each other.

ADDISON

This must be, at long last, our formal introduc-
tion. Until now we have met only in passing . . .

MISS CASWELL
That's how you met me. In passing.

MARGO
(smiles)
Eve, this is an old friend of Mr. DeWitt's mother
— Miss Caswell, Miss Harrington . . .
(the two girls say hello)
Addison, I've been wanting you to meet Eve for
the longest time —

ADDISON

(murmurs)

It could only have been your natural timidity that kept you from mentioning it . . .

MARGO

You've heard of her great interest in the Theatre —

ADDISON

We have that in common.

MARGO

Then you two must have a long talk —

EVE

I'm afraid Mr. DeWitt would find me boring before too long.

MISS CASWELL

You won't bore him, honey. You won't even get to talk.

ADDISON

(icily)

Claudia dear, come closer.

(she does, and he points)

Do you see that little man? He is Max Fabian. He is a producer. Go do yourself some good.

MISS CASWELL

(sighs)

Why do they always look like unhappy rabbits?

ADDISON

Because that is what they are. Go make him happy.

Miss Caswell drapes her coat over the rail, heads for Max. Addison puts Eve's arm in his.

ADDISON
(to Margo)
You mustn't worry about your little charge. She is in safe hands.

MARGO

Amen.

Eve smiles uncertainly at Margo as he leads her away. Margo looks after them. She downs her drink . . .

DISSOLVE TO:

MARGO'S LIVING ROOM — NIGHT

It's many Martinis later. Most of the guests have gone. The party has reached that static state — everyone's assumed more or less permanent places.

Birdie passes, carrying a cup of coffee. CAMERA FOLLOWS her to the piano where Margo sits on the bench beside the pianist. He is just finishing "Liebestraum" and she stares moodily into a Martini. Birdie halts beside her with the coffee. Margo looks up. Birdie holds out the coffee. Margo takes the onion out of the Martini, drops

it into the coffee and waves Birdie away. Birdie goes.
"Liebestraum" comes to an end. The pianist tries to ease
into a more sophisticated rhythm. Margo stops him.

> MARGO
>
> (quietly)
> "Liebestraum."

> PIANIST
>
> I just played it.

> MARGO
>
> Play it again.

> PIANIST
>
> But that was the fourth straight time.

> MARGO
>
> Then this will be five. I suppose you think I'm
> too drunk to count.

> PIANIST
>
> No. You're just crazy about "Liebestraum."

> MARGO
>
> "Liebestraum."

> PIANIST
>
> Look, Miss Channing . . . it's kind of depressing.
> If you don't mind my saying so, everybody's kind
> of dying on the vine . . .

206

MARGO

My dear Horowitz. In the first place, I'm paying
you union scale. Second, it's my piano. Third, if
everybody doesn't like kind of dying on the
vine, they can get off the vine and go home.
"Liebestraum."

Unhappily, he plays "Liebestraum." Margo sips her
Martini, stares down into it again. Bill tiptoes up.

BILL

(whispers)
Many of your guests have been wondering when
they may be permitted to view the body. Where
has it been laid out?

MARGO

(somberly)
It hasn't been laid out; we haven't finished with
the embalming. As a matter of fact, you're looking at it. The remains of Margo Channing. Sitting
up. It is my last wish to be buried sitting up.

BILL

(trying to kid her out of it)
Wouldn't you feel more natural taking a bow?

MARGO

You know nothing about feelings, natural or
unnatural.

207

Then without feelings, your guests were also wondering whether the music couldn't be a shade more on the — shall we say, happier side.

MARGO

If my guests do not like it here, I suggest they accompany you to the nursery where I'm sure you will all feel more at home.

Bill is about to get mad — when Max bustles up.

MAX

Margo. You by any chance got bicarbonate of soda in the house?

MARGO
(sympathetic)
Poor Max. Heartburn?
(Max nods)
It's that Miss Caswell. I don't know why she doesn't give Addison heartburn.

BILL

No heart to burn.

MARGO

Everybody has a heart — except some people.
(she finishes her drink, stands up)
Of course I've got bicarb. There's a box in the

pantry. We'll put your name on it. Max Fabian. It'll stay there. Always. Just for you.

MAX

(touched)

Let the rest of the world beat their brains out for a buck. It's friends that count. And I got friends.

MARGO

I love you, Max. I really mean it. I love you. Come to the pantry.

She takes off. Max waits to set Bill straight.

MAX

She loves me like a father. Also, she's loaded.

He starts after Margo. As the CAMERA PANS with Bill we see Margo going into the pantry with Max following her. Bill joins Addison and Miss Caswell on the stairs.

PANTRY — NIGHT

It's a good-sized one. Margo crosses to a cupboard. She finds the bicarb.

MARGO

Here you are, Maxie dear. One good burp and you'll be rid of that Miss Caswell . . .

MAX

The situation I'm in ain't the kind you can belch your way out of. I made a promise . . .

209

MARGO

To Miss Caswell?

(Max nods)

What?

MAX

An audition for the part we're replacing. What's-
her-name, your sister . . .

He adds water to the bicarb.

MARGO

Well, if she can act, she might not be bad. She
looks like she might burn down a plantation . . .

MAX

(mixing)
I feel right now like there's one burning in me.

MARGO

When's the audition?

MAX

A couple of weeks.

MARGO

I tell you what. Why don't I read with her?

MAX

Would you?

MARGO

Anything to help you out, Max.

MAX

(drinking)

This is real co-operation. I appreciate it.

MARGO

Not at all. And you could do me a big favor, if
you would —

MAX

All you got to do is name it.

MARGO

Give Eve Harrington a job in your office.

Max burps.

MARGO

You get quick action, don't you?

MAX

Margo, I wouldn't think of taking that girl away
from you . . .

MARGO

You said yourself my inventory is in good shape —
all of my merchandise put away. To keep her here
with nothing to do — I'd be standing in her way
. . . and you need her, Max.

MAX

But what could she do?

211

MARGO

She'd be a great help — read scripts, interview people you have to see, get rid of the ones you don't
have to . . . you'd be a man of leisure —

MAX

Well . . .

MARGO

Think of your health, Max — more time to relax,
play some cards.

MAX

I don't know if this would be a wise move . . .

MARGO

Promise.

MAX

I promise.

MARGO

(happily)
That's my Max.

Lloyd enters, looking for her.

LLOYD

There you are, both of you. Max, Karen has decided it's time to go . . .

MARGO

Where is she?

Up in your room.

MAX

If you'll excuse me —
                    (to Margo)
I'll go tell Miss Caswell . . .

MARGO

Watch out for heartburn.

MAX

I ain't worried so much now. It's nearly time for
my powder.

He goes out. A pause.

MARGO

Who's left out there?

LLOYD

Too many. And you've got a new guest. A movie
star from Hollywood.

MARGO

Shucks. And my autograph book is at the cleaners.

Another pause.

MARGO

You disapprove of me when I'm like this, don't
you?

213

LLOYD

Not exactly. Sometimes, though, I wish I understood you better.

MARGO

When you do, let me in on it.

LLOYD

I will.

Another pause.

MARGO

How's the new one coming?

LLOYD

The play? All right, I guess . . .

MARGO

"Cora." She's — still a girl of twenty?

LLOYD

Twentyish. It isn't important.

MARGO

Don't you think it's about time it became important?

LLOYD

How do you mean?

MARGO

Don't be evasive.

LLOYD

Margo, you haven't got any age.

MARGO

Miss Channing is ageless. Spoken like a press agent.

LLOYD

I know what I'm talking about. After all, they're my plays . . .

MARGO

Spoken like an author.

(abruptly)

Lloyd, I'm not twentyish. I am not thirtyish. Three months ago, I was forty years old. Forty. Four oh.

(she smiles)

That slipped out, I hadn't quite made up my mind to admit it. Now I feel as if I'd suddenly taken all my clothes off . . .

LLOYD

Week after week, to thousands of people, you're as young as you want . . .

MARGO

. . . as young as they want, you mean. And I'm not interested in whether thousands of people think I'm six or six hundred —

215

Just one person. Isn't that so?

(Margo doesn't answer)

You know what this is all about, don't you? It has very little to do with whether you should play "Cora" — it has everything to do with the fact you've had another fight with Bill.

A pause. Margo closes the box of bicarb.

MARGO

Bill's thirty-two. He looks thirty-two. He looked it five years ago, he'll look it twenty years from now. I hate men.

(she puts the box down)

Don't worry, Lloyd. I'll play your play. I'll wear rompers and come in rolling a hoop if you like . . .

MARGO'S BEDROOM — NIGHT

The bed is littered with fur coats. Karen is making repairs at Margo's dressing table. Eve enters, carrying a magnificent sable coat which she drops on the bed.

KAREN

Now who'd show up at this hour? It's time people went home — hold that coat up . . .

(Eve holds it up. Karen whistles)

. . . whose is it?

216

EVE

Some Hollywood movie star. Her plane got in late.

KAREN

Discouraging, isn't it? Women with furs like that where it never even gets cold . . .

EVE

Hollywood.

KAREN

Tell me, Eve — how are things going with you? Happy?

Eve melts into warmth. She beams, sits on the bed. Karen has spun around on the dressing-table stool.

EVE

There should be a new word for happiness. Being here with Miss Channing has been — I just can't say, she's been so wonderful, done so much for me —

KAREN

(smiles)

Lloyd says Margo compensates for underplaying on the stage by overplaying reality . . .

(she gets up, gets her own coat)

. . . next to that sable, my new mink seems like an old bedjacket . . . you've done your share, Eve. You've worked wonders with Margo . . .

She starts out.

217

                              EVE
                        (hesitantly)
          Mrs. Richards . . .

                              KAREN
                        (pauses, smiles)
          Karen.

                              EVE
          Karen . . .
                        (she picks at the coverlet)
          . . . isn't it awful, I'm about to ask you for an-
          other favor — after all you've done already.

                              KAREN
                        (crosses to her)
          Nobody's done so much, Eve. You've got to stop
          thinking of yourself as one of the Hundred
          Neediest Cases . . . what is it?

                              EVE
          Well . . . Miss Channing's affairs are in such
          good shape . . . there isn't enough to keep me
          as busy as I should be, really — not that I'd even
          consider anything that would take me away from
          her . . . but the other day — when I heard Mr.
          Fabian tell Miss Channing that her understudy
          was going to have a baby, and they'd have to
          replace her . . .

          She looks down at the coverlet once more.

KAREN

You want to be Margo's new understudy . . .

EVE

I don't let myself think about it, even —
  (she looks up, rises as she speaks)
— but I do know the part so well, and every bit of
the staging, there'd be no need to break in a new
girl —
        (suddenly afraid, she sits)
— but suppose I had to go on one night? To an
audience that came to see Margo Channing. No,
I couldn't possibly . . .

KAREN

  (laughs)
Don't worry too much about that. Margo just
doesn't miss performances. If she can walk, crawl
or roll — she plays.

EVE

  (nods proudly)
The show must go on.

KAREN

No, dear. Margo must go on.
        (she sits beside Eve)
As a matter of fact, I see no reason why you
shouldn't be Margo's understudy . . .

219

EVE

Do you think Miss Channing would approve?

KAREN

I think she'd cheer.

EVE

But Mr. Richards and Mr. Sampson —

KAREN

They'll do as they're told.

Eve smiles a little. A pause.

EVE

Then — would you talk to Mr. Fabian about it?

KAREN

Of course.

EVE

You won't forget it?

KAREN

I won't forget.

EVE

I seem to be forever thanking you for something, don't I?

She hugs Karen, leaves. She nearly collides with Birdie on her way in.

BIRDIE

The bed looks like a dead animal act. Which one
is sables?

KAREN

(pointing)
But she just got here . . .

BIRDIE

She's on her way. With half the men in the joint.
(she holds up the coat)

It's only a fur coat . . .

KAREN

What did you expect — live sables?

BIRDIE

A diamond collar, gold sleeves — you know, picture people . . .

They start out.

KAREN

Bill says actors out there eat just as infrequently
as here —

BIRDIE

They can always grab oranges off trees. This you
can't do in Times Square . . .

Through the open door, we see them go down the stairs
and out of sight.

SECOND FLOOR LANDING AND STAIRS

CAMERA PULLS BACK with Karen and Birdie as they come down into the scene, until IT discloses Bill, Max, Addison, Miss Caswell — and, at the feet of Bill and Addison . . . Eve. They are all seated on the steps.

Birdie goes through and down the stairs to the first floor. Karen remains with the others.

Addison is holding forth:

> ADDISON
> Every now and then, some elder statesman of the theatre or cinema assures the public that actors and actresses are just plain folks. Ignoring the fact that their greatest attraction to the public is their complete lack of resemblance to normal human beings . . .

> MISS CASWELL
> (as Birdie and the sables pass)
> Now there's something a girl could make sacrifices for.

> BILL
> And probably has.

> MISS CASWELL
> Sable.

MAX

(to Miss Caswell)

Did you say sable — or Gable?

MISS CASWELL

Either one.

ADDISON

It is senseless to insist that theatrical folk are no different from the good people of Des Moines, Chillicothe or Liverpool. By and large we are concentrated gatherings of neurotics, egomaniacs, emotional misfits, and precocious children —

MAX

(to Bill)

Gable. Why a feller like that don't come East to do a play . . .

BILL

(nods)

He must be miserable, the life he lives out there —

ADDISON

These so-called abnormalities — they're our stock in trade, they make us actors, writers, directors, et cetera, in the first place —

MAX

Answer me this. What makes a man become a producer?

223

ADDISON

What makes a man walk into a lion cage with nothing but a chair?

MAX

This answer satisfies me a hundred per cent.

ADDISON

We all have abnormality in common. We are a breed apart from the rest of humanity, we theatre folk. We are the original displaced personalities . . .

BILL

(laughs; to Eve)

You won't have to read his column tomorrow — you just heard it. I don't agree, Addison . . .

ADDISON

That happens to be your particular abnormality.

BILL

Oh, I'll admit there's a screwball element in the theatre. It sticks out, it's got spotlights on it and a brass band. But it isn't basic, it isn't standard — if it were, the theatre couldn't survive . . .

MISS CASWELL

(to a passing butler)

Oh, waiter . . .

The butler goes right by.

ADDISON

That isn't a waiter, my dear. That's a butler.

MISS CASWELL

Well, I can't yell "Oh, butler," can I? Maybe
somebody's name is Butler . . .

ADDISON

You have a point. An idiotic one, but a point.

MISS CASWELL

I don't want to make trouble. All I want is a drink.

MAX

(getting up)
Leave me get you one . . .

MISS CASWELL

(pitching)
Oh, thank you, Mr. Fabian.

Max leaves with her empty glass.

ADDISON

Well done. I see your career rising in the East like
the sun . . .

(to Bill)
. . . you were saying?

BILL

I was saying that the theatre is nine-tenths hard
work. Work done the hard way — by sweat, appli-

225

cation and craftsmanship. I'll agree to this — that
to be a good actor, actress, or anything else in the
theatre, means wanting to be that more than anything else in the world . . .

EVE

(abruptly)

Yes. Yes, it does . . .

BILL

(goes on)

It means a concentration of ambition, desire and
sacrifice such as no other profession demands . . .
and I'll agree that the man or woman who accepts those terms can't be ordinary, can't be —
just someone. To give so much for almost always
so little . . .

Eve speaks almost as if unaware of what she says. She
looks at no one in particular, just off . . .

EVE

So little. So little, did you say? Why, if there's
nothing else — there's applause. I've listened, from
backstage, to people applaud. It's like — like waves
of love coming over the footlights and wrapping
you up. Imagine . . . to know, every night, that
different hundreds of people love you . . . they
smile, their eyes shine — you've pleased them, they

want you, you belong. Just that alone is worth anything . . .

She becomes aware of Addison's strange smile, of Bill's look of warm interest. She's embarrassed, she turns away — then scrambles to her feet as Margo approaches with Lloyd from the direction of the pantry.

Margo's fake smile fades as Eve gets up. She's unpleasant and depressed.

> MARGO
> Don't get up. And please stop acting as if I were the queen mother.

> EVE
> (hurt)
> I'm sorry, I didn't mean to —

> BILL
> (sharply)
> Outside of a beehive, Margo, your behavior would hardly be considered either queenly or motherly!

> MARGO
> You're *in* a beehive, pal, didn't you know? We're all busy little bees, full of stings, making honey day and night —
> (to Eve)
> — aren't we, honey?

KAREN

Margo, really . . .

MARGO

Please don't play governess, Karen. I haven't your
unyielding good taste; I wish I'd gone to Radcliffe
too but Father wouldn't hear of it — he needed
help at the notions counter . . .

(to Addison)

I'm being rude now, aren't I? Or should I say
"ain't I"?

ADDISON

You're maudlin and full of self-pity. You're magnificent.

Max has come up with Miss Caswell's drink.

LLOYD

How about calling it a night?

MARGO

And you pose as a playwright. A situation preg-
nant with possibilities — and all you can think of
is everybody go to sleep . . .

BILL

It's a good thought.

MARGO

It won't play.

228

KAREN

As a nonprofessional, I think it's an excellent idea.
Undramatic, but practical . . .

As she speaks, she makes her way to Lloyd's side.

MARGO

Happy little housewife . . .

BILL

Cut it out.

MARGO

This is my house, not a theatre! In my house
you're a guest, not a director —

KAREN

Then stop being a star — stop treating your guests
as your supporting cast!

ADDISON

Hear, hear . . .

LLOYD

Now let's not get into a big hassel —

KAREN

It's about time we did! It's about time Margo
realized that what's attractive on stage need not
necessarily be attractive off!

MARGO

(suddenly)

All right! I'm going to bed.

(to Bill)

You be the host. It's your party. Happy birthday, welcome home, and we-who-are-about-to-die-
salute-you . . .

She starts upstairs.

BILL

Need any help?

MARGO

(pauses, smiles)

To put me to bed? Take my clothes off, hold my
head, tuck me in, turn out the lights, tiptoe
out . . . ? Eve would. Wouldn't you, Eve?

EVE

If you'd like.

MARGO

I wouldn't like.

She goes out, exits out of sight. A pause. Miss Caswell
reaches up to take the drink out of Max's hand.

MAX

I forgot I had it.

MISS CASWELL

I didn't.

Bill gets up and goes after Margo.

ADDISON

Too bad. We'll miss the third act. They're going
to play it off stage.

Eve turns away abruptly, in sudden tears.

LLOYD

Coming?

KAREN

In a minute . . .

She crosses to Eve, puts an arm around her.

KAREN

You mustn't mind Margo too much, even if
I do . . .

EVE

But there must be some reason, something I've
done without knowing . . .

KAREN

The reason is Margo and don't try to figure it out.
Einstein couldn't.

EVE

If I thought I'd offended her, of all people —

KAREN

Eve. I'm fond of Margo, too. But I know Margo.

231

And every now and then there is nothing I want to do so much as to kick her right square in the pants.

                    EVE
          (smiles)
Well — if she's got to pick on someone, I'd just as soon it was me.

Karen smiles back. She joins Lloyd and Max.

                    LLOYD
     Max is going to drop us.

                    ADDISON
I've often wondered, Max, why you bother with a chauffeur and limousine in New York City.

                    MAX
In my case it's necessary. Too many taxi drivers write plays.

                    ADDISON
     And too many of them are produced.

                MISS CASWELL
     Let's go sit by the piano.

232

ADDISON

You have me confused with Dan Dailey. You go
sit by the piano.

            (to Eve)

And you come sit by me.

             (to the others)

Good night.

They laugh, say "good night," and start downstairs. As
Eve crosses to Addison:

EVE

Karen . . .

            (Karen pauses)

. . . you won't forget will you? What we talked
about before?

KAREN

         (smiles)

No, Eve. I won't forget.

She follows the men downstairs. CAMERA MOVES to a
CLOSEUP of an old engraving of Mrs. Siddons as "The
Tragic Muse" which hangs among other theatrical me-
mentos on the stair wall . . .

                        FADE OUT

FADE IN

NEW YORK THEATRE — DAY

Margo gets out of a cab in front of the theatre and goes
in. It's a Friday afternoon — no performance.

LOBBY AND FOYER — DAY

Margo comes from the street through the lobby (a few
people buying tickets) and into the deserted foyer. She
spots Addison sprawled on one of the sofas.

> MARGO
>
> Why so remote, Addison? I should think you'd
> be at the side of your protégée, lending her moral
> support.

> ADDISON
>
> Miss Caswell, at the moment, is where I can lend
> no support — moral or otherwise.

> MARGO
>
> The ladies' — shall we say — lounge?

> ADDISON
>
> Being violently ill to her tummy.

> MARGO
>
> It's good luck before an audition. She'll be all
> right once it starts.

234

She heads for the auditorium.

ADDISON

Miss Caswell got lucky too late. The audition
is over.

MARGO

(stops)
Over? It can't be. I've come to read with her.
I promised Max.

ADDISON

The audition was called for 2:30. It is now nearly
four.

MARGO

(lightly)
Is it really? I must start wearing a watch, I never
do, you know . . . who read with Miss Caswell?
Bill?
(he shakes his head)
Lloyd?
(he shakes his head)
Well, it couldn't have been Max! Who?

ADDISON

Naturally enough, your understudy.

MARGO

I consider it highly unnatural to allow a girl in
an advanced state of pregnancy —

I refer to your new and unpregnant understudy.
Eve Harrington.

MARGO

Eve! My understudy . . .

ADDISON

(keenly)
Didn't you know?

MARGO

(quickly)
Of course I knew.

ADDISON

It just slipped your mind.

A moment of silence.

MARGO

How . . . how was Miss Caswell?

ADDISON

Frankly, I don't remember.

MARGO

Just slipped your mind.

ADDISON

Completely. Nor, I am sure, could anyone else
present tell you how Miss Caswell read, or whether
Miss Caswell read or rode a pogo stick . . .

MARGO

Was she that bad?

As Addison speaks, he rises with excitement.

ADDISON

Margo, as you know, I have lived in the Theatre as a Trappist monk lives in his faith. I have no other world, no other life — and once in a great while I experience that moment of Revelation for which all true believers wait and pray. You were one. Jeanne Eagels another . . . Paula Wessely . . . Hayes — there are others, three or four. Eve Harrington will be among them . . .

MARGO

(flatly)

I take it she read well.

ADDISON

It wasn't a reading, it was a performance. Brilliant, vivid, something made of music and fire . . .

MARGO

How nice.

ADDISON

In time she'll be what you are.

MARGO

A mass of music and fire. That's me. An old kazoo and some sparklers. Tell me — was Bill swept away, too, or were you too full of Revelation to notice?

ADDISON

Bill didn't say — but Lloyd was beside himself. He listened to his play as if someone else had written it, he said. It sounded so fresh, so new, so full of meaning . . .

MARGO

How nice for Lloyd. And how nice for Eve. How nice for everybody.

Addison, of course, knows exactly what he's doing. He senses the approaching typhoon, he whips it up.

ADDISON

Eve was incredibly modest. She insisted that no credit was due her, that Lloyd felt as he did only because she read his lines exactly as he had written them.

MARGO

The implication being that I have not been reading them as written?

ADDISON

To the best of my recollection, neither your name nor your performance entered the conversation.

Miss Caswell appears, uncertainly, in the background.

238

ADDISON

Feeling better, my dear?

MISS CASWELL

Like I just swam the English Channel. Now what?

ADDISON

Your next move, it seems to me, should be toward television.

Margo, abruptly, starts for the auditorium. Addison smiles. He takes Miss Caswell's arm.

MISS CASWELL

Tell me this. Do they have auditions for television?

ADDISON

That's all television is, my dear. Nothing but auditions.

He leads her toward the street.

THEATRE

The curtain is up; the set, covered, is a bedroom in a deteriorating Southern mansion.

There is no one in the theatre but Max, seated on the aisle about two-thirds down, and Eve with Lloyd and Bill on the stage. She is seated; they stand between her and the auditorium. There is some ad-lib talk among the three which we cannot make out. CAMERA is on Margo marching down the aisle with a steady pace.

239

She passes Max who smiles a sickly, hopeful smile. She ignores him as if he were a used paper cup. She disappears through the door which leads backstage.

Max whistles. Lloyd turns. Max indicates the door and puts his hands to his head in despair.

Margo walks out of the wings on stage. Bill and Lloyd turn to her. Eve rises.

> MARGO
> (cheerily)
> Terribly sorry I'm late, lunch was long and I couldn't find a cab — where's Miss Caswell, shall we start? Oh, hello, Eve . . .

> EVE
> Hello, Miss Channing.

> MARGO
> How are you making out in Mr. Fabian's office?
> (over the footlights to Max)
> I don't want you working the child too hard, Max — just because you promised. As you see, I kept my promise, too . . .

Max slumps in his seat. By the time Margo turns back to them, the others have exchanged swift looks.

> BILL
> It's all over.

MARGO

What's all over?

BILL

The audition. Eve read with Miss Caswell.

MARGO

(pleased astonishment)

Eve?

(she turns to her)

How enchanting.

(to Lloyd and Bill)

Wherever did you two get the idea of having Eve read with Miss Caswell?

LLOYD

She's your understudy.

MARGO

Eve? Eve, my understudy? But I had no idea . . .

LLOYD

I thought you knew. She was put on over a week ago —

MARGO

It seems almost inconceivable that I haven't seen her backstage, but with so many people loitering about . . . well, well. So Eve is not working for Max after all —

(out to Max again)

— Max, you sly puss.

241

Max submerges further in his seat.

EVE

Miss Channing, I can't tell you how glad I am that you arrived so late.

MARGO

Really, Eve? Why?

EVE

Well, if you'd been here to begin with, I wouldn't have dared to read at all . . .

MARGO

Why not?

EVE

. . . and if you'd come in the middle, I'd have stopped, I couldn't have gone on —

MARGO

(murmurs)

What a pity, all that fire and music being turned off . . .

BILL

What fire and music?

MARGO

You wouldn't understand.
(to Lloyd)
How was Miss Caswell?

LLOYD

Back to the Copacabana. But Eve. Margo, let me tell you about Eve —

EVE

(breaking in)
I was dreadful, Miss Channing, believe me — I have no right to be anyone's understudy, much less yours . . .

MARGO

I'm sure you underestimate yourself, Eve. You always do.
(to Lloyd)
You were about to tell me about Eve . . .

LLOYD

You'd have been proud of her.

MARGO

I'm sure . . .

LLOYD

She was a revelation . . .

MARGO

To you, too?

LLOYD

What do you mean?

243

MARGO

(the ice begins to form)

I mean, among other things, that it must have
been a revelation to have your twenty-four-year-old
character played by a twenty-four-year-old actress.

LLOYD

That's beside the point.

MARGO

It's right to the point. Also that it must have
sounded so new and fresh to you — so exciting to
have the lines read just as you wrote them!

BILL

Addison — !

MARGO

So full of meaning, fire and music!

LLOYD

You've been talking to that venomous fishwife,
Addison DeWitt —

MARGO

— in this case, apparently, as trustworthy as the
World Almanac!

LLOYD

You knew when you came in that the audition
was over, that Eve was your understudy! Playing
that childish little game of cat-and-mouse . . .

244

MARGO

Not mouse, never mouse! If anything — rat!

LLOYD

You have a genius for making a barroom brawl out of a perfectly innocent misunderstanding at most!

MARGO

Perfectly innocent! Men have been hanged for less! I'm lied to, attacked behind my back, accused of reading your silly dialogue inaccurately — as if it were Holy Gospel!

LLOYD

I never said it was!

MARGO

When you listened as if someone else had written your play — whom did you have in mind? Sherwood? Arthur Miller? Beaumont and Fletcher?

Max has edged his way to the stage.

MAX

(from below)
May I say a word?

LLOYD

No!

(to Margo)
What makes you think that either Miller or

245

Sherwood would stand for the nonsense I take from you — you'd better stick to Beaumont and Fletcher! They've been dead for three hundred years!

He stalks into the wings. Bill's reaction to the fight is typical. He lights a cigarette, stretches out on the covered bed. Eve stands frozen with fear. Margo yells after Lloyd into the wings.

> MARGO
>
> And they're getting better performances today than they ever got! *All* playwrights should be dead for three hundred years!

Lloyd comes out of the door leading to the auditorium. The battle goes on without a pause. As he yells back, he crosses to Max at row A, center.

> LLOYD
>
> That would solve none of their problems — because actresses never die! The stars never die and never change!

He starts up the aisle with Max.

> MARGO
>
> You can change this star any time you want! For a new, fresh, exciting one fully equipped with fire and music! Any time you want — starting with tonight's performance!

246

Now it's Max who stops and shouts back at her.

MAX

This is for lawyers to talk about, this concerns a run-of-the-play contract, and this you can't rewrite or ad lib!

MARGO

(from the stage)

Are you threatening me with legal action, Mr. Fabian?

MAX

Are you breaking the contract?

MARGO

Answer my question!

MAX

Who am I to threaten? I'm a dying man.

MARGO

I didn't hear you!

MAX

(yelling)

I said I'm a dying man!

MARGO

Not until the last drugstore has sold its last pill!

LLOYD

(from the top of the aisle)

I shall never understand the weird process by

which a body with a voice suddenly fancies itself as a mind! Just when exactly does an actress decide they're *her* words she's saying and *her* thoughts she's expressing?

                    MARGO
Usually at the point when she's got to rewrite and re-think them to keep the audience from leaving the theatre!

                    LLOYD
It's about time the piano realized it has not written the concerto!

Max has already walked out unhappily. Lloyd now slams out. Margo glares after him, then turns to Bill who smokes his cigarette peacefully on the bed.

                    MARGO
          (quiet menace)
And you, I take it, are the Paderewski who plays his concerto on me, the piano?
          (Bill waves his cigarette; he's noncommittal)
Where is Princess Fire-and-Music?

                    BILL
Who?

                    MARGO
The kid. Junior.

BILL

       (looks lazily)

Gone.

MARGO

I must have frightened her away.

BILL

I wouldn't be surprised. Sometimes you frighten me.

MARGO

       (paces up and down)

Poor little flower. Just dropped her petals and folded her tent . . .

BILL

Don't mix your metaphors.

MARGO

I'll mix what I like.

BILL

Okay. Mix.

MARGO

I'm nothing but a body with a voice. No mind.

BILL

What a body, what a voice.

MARGO

That ex-ship news reporter. No body, no voice, *all* mind!

BILL

The gong rang. The fight's over. Calm down.

MARGO

I will not calm down!

BILL

Don't calm down.

MARGO

You're being terribly tolerant, aren't you?

BILL

I'm trying terribly hard.

MARGO

Well, you needn't. I will not be tolerated. And I
will not be plotted against!

BILL

Here we go . . .

MARGO

Such nonsense, what do you all take me for —
little Nell from the country? Been my understudy
for over a week without my knowing, carefully
hidden no doubt —

BILL
(sits up)
Now don't get carried away —

MARGO
(going right on)
— shows up for an audition when everyone knew

250

I'd be here . . . and gives a performance! Out of
nowhere — gives a performance!

BILL

You've been all through that with Lloyd —

MARGO

The playwright doesn't make the performance —
and it doesn't just happen! And this one didn't
— full of fire and music and what-not, it was carefully rehearsed I have no doubt, over and over, full
of those Bill Sampson touches!

BILL

I am sick and tired of these paranoiac outbursts!

MARGO

Paranoiac!

BILL

I didn't know Eve Harrington was your understudy until half past two this afternoon!

MARGO

Tell that to Dr. Freud! Along with the rest of
it . . .

She turns away. Bill grabs her, pulls her down on the bed.
He holds her down.

BILL

No, I'll tell it to you! For the last time, I'll tell it
to you. Because you've got to stop hurting your-

self, and me, and the two of us by these paranoiac tantrums!

MARGO
(struggling)
That word again! I don't even know what it
means . . .

BILL
(firmly)
It's about time you found out. I love you.
(Margo says "Ha!")
I love you. You're a beautiful and intelligent
woman —
(Margo says "A body with a voice")
— a beautiful and intelligent woman and a great
actress —
(he waits. Margo says nothing)
— at the peak of her career. You have every reason
for happiness —
(Margo says "Except happiness")
— every reason, but due to some strange, uncon-
trollable, unconscious drive you permit the slightest action of a kid —
(Margo sneers "Kid!")
— kid like Eve to turn you into an hysterical,
· screaming harpy! Now once and for all, stop it!

Margo seems quiet. He gets up. She sits up.

MARGO

It's obvious you're not a woman.

BILL

I've been aware of that for some time.

MARGO

Well, I am.

BILL

I'll say.

MARGO

Don't be condescending.

BILL

Come on, get up. I'll buy you a drink.

MARGO

(with dignity)

I admit I may have seen better days, but I am still
not to be had for the price of a cocktail — like a
salted peanut.

BILL

(laughs)

Margo, let's make peace.

MARGO

The terms are too high. Unconditional surrender.

BILL

Just being happy? Just stopping all this nonsense
about Eve — and Eve and me?

MARGO

It's not nonsense.

BILL

But if I tell you it is — as I just did. Were you listening to me?

(Margo nods)

Isn't that enough?

MARGO

I wish it were.

BILL

Then what would be enough?

(Margo doesn't answer)

If we got married?

MARGO

I wouldn't want you to marry me just to prove something.

BILL

You've had so many reasons for not wanting to marry me . . . Margo, tell me what's behind all this.

MARGO

I — I don't know, Bill. Just a feeling, I don't know . . .

BILL

I think you do know but you won't or can't tell me.

254

(Margo doesn't say)

I said before it was going to be my last try, and I meant it. I can't think of anything else to do. I wish I could.

(a pause)

We usually wind up screaming and throwing things as the curtain comes down. Then it comes up again and everything's fine. But not this time.

(he takes a breath)

You know there isn't a playwright in the world who could make me believe this would happen between two adult people. Good-bye, Margo.

No word from her. He starts away.

MARGO

Bill . . .

(he stops)

. . . where are you going? To find Eve?

BILL

(smiles grimly)

That suddenly makes the whole thing believable.

He goes out. Margo, alone, sits for a moment sadly. Then she begins to cry . . .

FADE OUT

255

FADE IN

RICHARDS' STUDIO APARTMENT — DAY

One large room, a small foyer with a door to the corridor.
A stair up one wall to a narrow balcony from which a
couple of bedrooms open.

Karen is painting. Earnestly but badly. A still life of an
orange, an avocado, an eggplant and three bananas.

> KAREN'S VOICE
> *On the day of the audition, my biggest worry was*
> *to keep a banana from looking like part of an egg-*
> *plant . . . then Lloyd came home.*
>   (in the background, Lloyd lets himself in)
> *It was right after his brawl with Margo . . .*

Lloyd slams the door, flings his hat away, strides in, peeling off muffler and overcoat.

> KAREN
> Lloyd, what's happened?

> LLOYD
> Up to here! That's where I've got it — up to here!
> Of all the star-ridden, presumptuous, hysterical —

> KAREN
> Margo, again . . .

256

LLOYD

And again and again! Two hours late for the audition, to begin with —

KAREN

That's on time for Margo.

LLOYD

Then a childish, heavy-handed routine about not knowing Eve was her understudy —

KAREN

It's just possible she didn't . . .

LLOYD

Of course she knew! For one thing, Addison told her how superbly Eve had read the part — !
     (suddenly softening)
Karen, let me tell you about Eve. She's got everything — a born actress. Sensitive, understanding, young, exciting, vibrant —

KAREN

— don't run out of adjectives, dear.

LLOYD

— everything a playwright first thinks of wanting to write about . . . until his play becomes a vehicle for Miss Channing.

KAREN

Margo hasn't done badly by it.

257

Margo. Margo's great. She knows it. That's the trouble. She can play Peck's Bad Boy all she wants, and who's to stop her? Who's to give her that boot in the rear she needs and deserves?

He starts up the stairs to a bedroom.

KAREN

(murmurs)

It's going to be a cozy week-end.

LLOYD

(pauses)

What is?

KAREN

We're driving out to the country tomorrow night. Just the four of us. Bill, Margo, you and I . . .

LLOYD

Well. We've spent week-ends before with nobody talking . . .

(continues up the stairs)

. . . just be sure to lock up all blunt instruments and throwable objects.

As he goes into one of the bedrooms, Karen sits thoughtfully on a couch. She muses . . .

KAREN'S VOICE

Newton—they say, thought of gravity by getting

hit on the head by an apple. And the man who
invented the steam engine, he was watching a tea-
kettle . . . but not me. My Big Idea came to me
just sitting on a couch . . .

She lies down, folds her hands behind her head.

KAREN'S VOICE

That boot in the rear to Margo. Heaven knows
she had one coming. From me, from Lloyd, from
Eve, Bill, Max, and so on — we'd all felt those size
fives of hers often enough . . . but how? The
answer was buzzing around me like a fly . . .

She sits up. She smiles. The smile fades . . .

KAREN'S VOICE

I had it. But I let it go. Screaming and calling
names is one thing — but this could mean . . .

She shakes her head, crosses to her easel, resumes work on
the bananas. She slows down, then stops.

KAREN'S VOICE

Why not? Why, I said to myself, not? It would
all seem perfectly legitimate. And there were only
two people in the world who would know. Also,
the boot would land where it would do the most
good for all concerned —

She puts the brush away and crosses to the phone which
is by Lloyd's work chair. As she crosses:

259

KAREN'S VOICE

And after all, it was no more than a perfectly harm-
less joke which Margo, herself, would be the first
to enjoy . . .

She looks in a leather phone book, picks up the phone
and dials.

KAREN'S VOICE

. . . and no reason why she shouldn't be told about
it — in time.

There's an answer at the other end.

KAREN

(into phone)

Hello . . . will you call Miss Eve Harrington to
the phone, please? Not at all . . . thank you.

And as she waits, we

DISSOLVE TO:

COUNTRYSIDE — NIGHT

Open country. Preferably no houses in sight. Plenty of
snow. Lloyd's car drives along.

KAREN'S VOICE

It was a cold week-end — outside and in. Bill
didn't come at all. Margo didn't know where he
was and didn't care — she kept saying. Somehow
we staggered through Sunday — and by the time

*we drove Margo to the station late Monday after-
noon, she and Lloyd had thawed out to the extent
of being civil to each other . . .*

INSIDE LLOYD'S COUPE — NIGHT

Lloyd driving. All three in the front seat.

KAREN

What time is it?

LLOYD

When you asked a minute ago it was five-forty-
two. It is now five-forty-three. When you ask
again a minute from now, it will be —

KAREN

I just don't want Margo to miss her train. As it
is, she'll barely make the theatre . . .

LLOYD

Five-fifty-five. We'll be at the station in plenty of
time.

MARGO

That little place just two hours from New York.
It's on my list of things-I'll-never-understand. Like
collecting shrunken Indian heads . . .

KAREN

Of all people you should know what it means to
want some peace and quiet —

261

MARGO

Peace and quiet is for libraries.

The car swerves — suddenly and slightly.

KAREN

Lloyd, be careful . . .

LLOYD

Just a little skid, that's all. This road's like glass.

MARGO

Karen and I just don't want an accident —

LLOYD

I have no intention of having an accident!

MARGO

It's not important whether you do. We are wearing long underwear.

They all laugh. Suddenly the car slows and stops — with that hissing sound that can mean only one thing — no gas.

LLOYD

Now what's this . . . ?

He tries to start it again. No luck. He turns on the dashboard lights. The gas gauge reads empty.

LLOYD

But it can't be! We can't be out of gas! I filled it myself yesterday!

262

> (to Karen)

Wasn't it full when you drove to Brewster this morning?

                    KAREN
> (very low)

I guess I didn't look. You know I don't pay attention to those things . . .

                    LLOYD

Incredible . . .

Futilely, he runs the starter again.

                    MARGO
> (crisply)

How much time have we?

                    LLOYD

Roughly ten minutes.

                    MARGO

How far to the station?

                    LLOYD

Three or four miles . . .

                    MARGO

Any houses or farms around where we can borrow gas?

                    LLOYD
> (looking)

None in sight, there aren't many along this back road . . .

MARGO

Not many cars either, not much chance of a
lift . . .

A moment of silence.

LLOYD

Well. No sense my just sitting here. I'm going to
walk up about half a mile, just in case.

He starts out of the car. The cold comes in like a knife,
the women react.

KAREN

You'll break your neck on that ice.

LLOYD

(grins)

What a way to die — trying to get an actress to the
theatre in time. Tell Max I want to be buried with
my royalties . . .

KAREN

Don't joke about such things.

MARGO

(quietly)

How fortunate that I have an understudy so ready,
so willing and so able to go on.

LLOYD

The audience will want its money refunded, believe me.

264

Thank you, Lloyd. Godspeed.

Lloyd starts down the road. He slips once, recovers, waves and keeps going.

KAREN

He always looks so pathetic whenever he does anything physical —

MARGO

It seems to me that walking, for most people, is not very dangerous.

KAREN

(smiles)

I just never think of Lloyd as anywhere but indoors and anything but sitting down.

MARGO

Be brave. He'll come back — with or without gas.

They tuck the fur car robe about them. A pause. Margo turns on the radio . . . it's "Liebestraum."

MARGO

Do you want it on?

KAREN

It doesn't matter.

MARGO

I detest cheap sentiment.

She turns it off. Another pause.

MARGO

Karen.

(Karen says "hm?")

I haven't been very pleasant this week-end.

KAREN

We've all seemed a little tense lately . . .

MARGO

Come to think of it, I haven't been very pleasant for weeks. For that, I'm truly sorry. More than any two people I know, I don't want you and Lloyd to be angry with me . . .

KAREN

We're never deeply angry, we just get sore. The way you do. We know you too well . . .

MARGO

So many people — know me. I wish I did. I wish someone would tell me about me . . .

KAREN

You're Margo. Just — Margo.

MARGO

And what is that? Besides something spelled out in light bulbs, I mean. Besides something called a temperament, which consists mostly of swooping about on a broomstick screaming at the top of my voice . . . infants behave the way I do, you know. They carry on and misbehave — they'd get

266

drunk if they knew how — when they can't have what they want. When they feel unwanted or insecure — or unloved . . .

There's a pause.

KAREN

What about Bill?

MARGO

What about Bill?

KAREN

He's in love with you.

MARGO

More than anything in this world, I love Bill. And I want Bill. I want him to want me. But me. Not Margo Channing. And if I can't tell them apart — how can he?

KAREN

Why should he — and why should you?

MARGO

Bill's in love with Margo Channing. He's fought with her, worked with her, loved her . . . but ten years from now — Margo Channing will have ceased to exist. And what's left will be . . . what?

KAREN

Margo. Bill is all of eight years younger than you.

267

MARGO

Those years stretch as the years go on. I've seen it
happen too often.

KAREN

Not to you. Not to Bill.

MARGO

Isn't that what they always say?

She turns the radio on again. A piano nocturne . . .

MARGO

I don't suppose the heater runs when the motor
doesn't?

KAREN

Silly, isn't it? You'd think they'd fix it so people
could just sit in a car and keep warm . . .

Margo nods, gets some cigarettes out of her bag. She
offers one to Karen. They light up.

MARGO

About Eve. I've acted pretty disgracefully toward
her, too.

KAREN

Well . . .

MARGO

Let's not fumble for excuses, not here and now
with my hair down. At best, let's say I've been
oversensitive to . . . well, to the fact that she's so

young — so feminine and helpless. To so many things I want to be for Bill . . . funny business, a woman's career. The things you drop on your way up the ladder, so you can move faster. You forget you'll need them again when you go back to being a woman. That's one career all females have in common — whether we like it or not — being a woman. Sooner or later we've got to work at it, no matter what other careers we've had or wanted . . . and, in the last analysis, nothing is any good unless you can look up just before dinner or turn around in bed — and there he is. Without that, you're not a woman. You're something with a French provincial office or a book full of clippings — but you're not a woman . . .

> (she smiles at Karen)

. . . slow curtain. The end.

A pause. There are tears in Karen's eyes.

KAREN

Margo.

> (she hesitates)

Margo, I want you to know how sorry I am about this . . .

MARGO

About what?

KAREN

(indicating their predicament)

This. I can't tell you how sorry I am!

MARGO

Don't give it a thought, one of destiny's merry pranks. After all, you didn't personally drain the gasoline out of the tank . . .

She snuggles down into her furs. Karen flashes an unhappy look at her. She, too, snuggles down . . .

DISSOLVE TO:

THEATRE ALLEY — NIGHT

The snow has been shoveled to either side of the alley, making a lane. The performance is just over.

Addison, his back to us, stands looking toward the stage door. A few actors, on their way out.

ADDISON'S VOICE

Eve, of course, was superb. Many of the audience understandably preferred to return another time to see Margo. But those who remained cheered loudly, lustily and long for Eve . . . how thoughtful of her to call and invite me — that afternoon . . .

He starts to walk toward the stage door.

270

... and what a happy coincidence that several
representatives of other newspapers happened to
be present. All of us — invited that afternoon to
attend an understudy's performance ...

He goes in the stage door.

THEATRE—BACKSTAGE

More activity than last time, the performance being just
over. Addison comes through the door, picks his way
toward Margo's dressing room:

ADDISON'S VOICE

... about which the management knew nothing
until they were forced to ring up the curtain at
nine o'clock. Coincidence. Also every indication
of intrigue, skulduggery and fraud ...

The door to the dressing room is open just a bit. Addison
pauses beside the open door to listen.

BILL'S VOICE

(from within)

... you were better than all right, kid, you gave a
performance, you rang a bell —

Addison uses his cane to swing the door open further, so
that both he and we can see as well as hear.

MARGO'S DRESSING ROOM

Bill faces Eve, who wears Margo's costume. She is a
ravishing sight. Her eyes shine up to his radiantly.

271

BILL

(continuing)

— little things here and there, it doesn't matter. You can be proud of yourself, you've got a right to be.

EVE

(quietly)

Are you proud of me, Bill?

BILL

I'll admit I was worried when Max called. I had my doubts —

EVE

You shouldn't have had any doubts.

BILL

— after all, the other day was one scene, the woods are full of one-scene sensations. But you did it. With work and patience, you'll be a fine actress. If that's what you want to be.

EVE

Is that what you want me to be?

BILL

I'm talking about you. And what you want.

EVE

So am I.

BILL

What have I got to do with it?

272

Everything.

BILL

(lightly)

The names I've been called. But never Svengali.

(he pats her shoulder)

Good luck.

He starts out. Addison ducks.

EVE

Don't run away, Bill.

BILL

(stops)

From what would I be running?

EVE

You're always after truth — on the stage. What about off?

BILL

(curiously)

I'm for it.

EVE

Then face it. I have. Since that first night — here — in this dressing room.

BILL

(smiles)

When I told you what every young actress should know.

EVE

When you told me that whatever I became, it
would be because of you —

BILL

Your makeup's a little heavy.

EVE

— and for you.

BILL

(slowly)
You're quite a girl.

EVE

You think?

BILL

I'm in love with Margo. Hadn't you heard?

EVE

You hear all kinds of things . . .

BILL

I'm only human, rumors to the contrary. And I'm
as curious as the next man . . .

EVE

Find out.

BILL

(deliberately)
Only thing, what I go after, I want to go after. I
don't want it to come after me.

Tears come to Eve's eyes. She turns away slowly.

274

BILL

Don't cry. Just score it as an incomplete forward pass.

He walks out. Addison ducks to avoid being seen. Eve glares after Bill, tears the wig from her head, throws it on the dressing table. Her glance is caught by a pair of scissors. Swiftly, she snatches them up and in a sharp, vicious gesture she slashes the wig. Addison knocks politely at the door. Eve turns.

ADDISON

May I come in?

EVE

Certainly, Mr. DeWitt . . .

ADDISON

(entering)

I expected to find this little room overcrowded, with a theatre full of people at your feet . . .

EVE

I consider myself lucky they didn't throw things.

She starts creaming her face, removing makeup.

ADDISON

Of course your performance was no surprise to me. After the other day I regarded it as no more than — a promise fulfilled.

EVE

You're more than kind. But it's still Miss Chan-

ning's performance. I'm just a carbon copy you
read when you can't find the original . . .

ADDISON

You're more than modest.

EVE

It's not modesty. I just don't try to kid myself.

ADDISON

A revolutionary approach to the theatre. However,
if I may make a suggestion . . .

EVE

Please do.

ADDISON

I think the time has come for you to shed some
of your humility. It is just as false not to blow your
horn at all as it is to blow it too loudly.

EVE

I don't think I've done anything to sound off
about.

ADDISON

We all come into this world with our little egos
equipped with individual horns. If we don't blow
them — who will?

EVE

Even so. One isolated pretty good performance by
an understudy. It'll be forgotten tomorrow.

276

ADDISON

It needn't be.

EVE

Even if I wanted to — as you say — be less hum-
ble, blow my own horn . . . how would I do it?
I'm less than nobody.

ADDISON

I am somebody.

Eve rises. She eyes him steadily.

EVE

You certainly are.

She goes into the bathroom.

ADDISON

Leave the door open a bit, so we can talk.

Eve does so.

ADDISON

After you change, if you're not busy elsewhere,
we can have supper . . .

EVE

(from the bathroom)

I'd love to! Or should I pretend I'm busy?

ADDISON

(smiling)

Let's have a minimum of pretending. I'll want to
do a column about you —

277

EVE

I'm not enough for a paragraph.

ADDISON

— perhaps more than one. There's so much I want
to know. I've heard your story in bits and pieces
. . . your home in Wisconsin, your tragic marriage,
your fanatical attachment to Margo — it started in
San Francisco, didn't it?
          (No answer. Addison smiles)
I say — your idolatry of Margo started in San Francisco, didn't it?

EVE

That's right.

ADDISON

San Francisco. An oasis of civilization in the California desert. Tell me, do you share my high
opinion of San Francisco?

EVE

Yes, I do.

ADDISON

And that memorable night when Margo first
dazzled you from the stage — which theatre was it
in San Francisco? Was it — the Shubert?

EVE

          (a slight pause)
Yes. The Shubert.

278

ADDISON
(grins happily)
A fine old theatre, the Shubert. Full of tradition,
untouched by the earthquake — so sorry — fire
. . . by the way, what was your husband's name?

EVE
Eddie . . .

ADDISON
Eddie what?

Eve sticks her head and naked shoulder around the door.

EVE
I'm about to go into the shower. I won't be able
to hear you . . .

ADDISON
It can wait. Where would you like to go? We'll
make this a special night . . .

EVE
(trustingly)
You take charge.

ADDISON
I believe I will.

She closes the door. He leans back, lights a cigarette.

DISSOLVE TO:

52ND STREET — NEW YORK — DAY

A cab drives up to "21."

> KAREN'S VOICE
>
> Some of the morning papers carried a little squib
> about Eve's performance. Not much, but full of
> praise . . . I couldn't imagine how they found out
> about it — but Lloyd said Max's publicity man
> probably sent out the story . . .

Karen gets out of the cab, pays and goes in.

> KAREN'S VOICE
>
> . . . at any rate, I felt terribly guilty and ashamed
> of myself — and wanted nothing so much as to
> forget the whole thing. Margo and I were having
> lunch at "21" — just like girl friends — with hats
> on . . .

LOBBY — "21" — DAY

Karen consults her watch and the doorman as she enters.

> KAREN
>
> Has Miss Channing come in?

> DOORMAN
>
> Not yet, Mrs. Richards.

Karen sees Eve, who waits as Addison hands his hat, coat
and cane to an attendant. She smiles, crosses to her.

> KAREN
>
> Eve. I've heard the most wonderful things about
> your performance —

280

EVE

Mostly relief that I managed to stagger through
it at all.

ADDISON

She was magnificent.

KAREN

(pleased)
Then you've heard, too.

ADDISON

I was there. An eye-witness.

KAREN

(staggered)
You were there? At the play — last night?

ADDISON

(smiles)
A happy coincidence.

EVE

(quickly)
We're having lunch with a movie-talent scout.

KAREN

They certainly don't waste much time.

EVE

Nothing definite yet — it's just to have lunch.

281

ADDISON

They'll be wasting this much of their time at any
rate. Eve has no intention of going to Hollywood.

He turns to Karen, changing the subject.

ADDISON

From the smartness of your dress, I take it your
luncheon companion is a lady?

KAREN

(smiles)

Margo.

ADDISON

Margo? Lunching in public?

KAREN

It's a new Margo. But she's just as late as the old
one.

ADDISON

She may be later than you think.

As he speaks, he crosses to pick up an evening paper,
opens it as he comes back.

ADDISON

(handing it to her)

Why not read my column to pass the time? The
minutes will fly like hours . . .

(he takes Eve's arm)

. . . and now we must join our sunburned eager
beaver.

He goes up the stairs with Eve. Karen glances after them curiously, then at the column. It is headed: "Things I Promised Not to Tell" by Addison DeWitt. Her expression becomes increasingly horrified. She drops the paper and rushes out . . .

DISSOLVE TO:

MARGO'S LIVING ROOM — DAY

Addison's column quivers in Margo's hand as she strides about, reading it. Karen sits miserably.

> MARGO
> (declaiming)
> ". . . my hat which has, lo, these many seasons become more firmly rooted about my ears, is lifted to Miss Harrington. I am once more available for dancing in the streets and shouting from the housetops" . . . I thought that one went out with Woollcott . . .
> (she skips part of the column)
> Down here . . . here, listen to this — ". . . Miss Harrington had much to tell — and these columns shall report her faithfully — about the lamentable practice in our theatre of permitting, shall we say — mature — actresses to continue playing roles requiring a youth and vigor of which they retain but a dim memory —"

KAREN

I just can't believe it.

MARGO

It gets better! "— about the understandable re-
luctance on the part of our entrenched First Ladies
of the Stage to encourage, shall we say — younger
— actresses; about Miss Harrington's own long
and unsupported struggle for opportunity —"

KAREN

I can't believe Eve said those things!

Margo crumples the paper as if it were Eve's neck.

MARGO

(pacing)

In this rat race, everybody's guilty till they're
proved innocent! One of the differences between
the Theatre and civilization . . .

(she hurls the paper away)

. . . what gets me is how all of the papers in town
happened to catch that particular performance!

KAREN

(weakly)

Lloyd says it's a publicity release.

MARGO

The little witch must have had Indian runners
out, snatching critics out of bars, steam rooms and

museums or wherever they hole up . . . well, she won't get away with it! Nor will Addison DeWitt and his poison pen! If Equity or my lawyer can't or won't do anything about it, I will personally stuff that pathetic little lost lamb down Mr. DeWitt's ugly throat . . .

She pauses in mid-air to look at . . . Bill. He has come up the stairs two at a time, stands at the landing.

> BILL
>
> (quietly)
>
> I came as soon as I read that piece of filth. I ran all the way . . .

Margo suddenly starts to cry. She turns from him. Bill takes her in his arms. He holds her . . .

> BILL
>
> Bill's here, baby. Everything's all right, now.

Margo says nothing, just hides in his embrace. He soothes her, pets her . . . he looks over at Karen.

> KAREN
>
> I guess at this point I'm what the French call de trop . . .

> BILL
>
> (smiles)
>
> Maybe just a little around the edges.

Karen smiles back, waves, and goes out.

DISSOLVE TO:

Karen's having some lunch. Lloyd, still in his robe, sits opposite her having some coffee and a cigarette. A copy of the interview before them.

> LLOYD
>
> (is saying)

— it's Addison, from start to finish, it drips with his brand of venom . . . taking advantage of a kid like that, twisting her words, making her say what he wanted her to say —

> KAREN

Where'd you get all that information?

> LLOYD
>
> (puts out his cigarette)

Eve.

> KAREN

Eve?

> LLOYD

She's been to see me, as a matter of fact she left just before you came in — you just missed her.

> KAREN

That was a pity . . .

286

LLOYD

(gets up)

She wanted to explain about the interview, wanted
to apologize to someone — and didn't dare face
Margo . . .

KAREN

I wonder why.

Lloyd wanders about — he seems to be searching for
words, for a position to maintain . . .

LLOYD

She started to tell me all about it — and she
couldn't finish, she cried so . . .

He's over by a window, his back to her. Karen eyes him
curiously, waiting for the payoff.

LLOYD

(finally)

You know, I've been going over our financial condition — if you'll pardon the expression.

KAREN

That's quite a change of subject.

LLOYD

(walks again)

What with taxes coming up — and since I'm a
playwright and not an oil-well operator — well,
I've been thinking . . .

KAREN

I'm trying hard to follow you.

LLOYD

If — instead of waiting until next season to do
Footsteps on the Ceiling, which is in pretty good
shape — and if Margo can be talked into going on
tour with *Aged in Wood* — we could put *Footsteps* into production right away . . .

KAREN

I'm beginning to catch up.

LLOYD

If we could cast it properly, that is . . .

KAREN

(carefully)

Maybe get some younger actress for the part?
Someone who'd look the part as well as play it?

LLOYD

(smiles)

You've got to admit it would be a novelty.

KAREN

Now you're quoting Addison. Or Eve.

A pause.

LLOYD

Eve did mention the play, you know. But just in

288

passing — she'd never ask to play a part like "Cora." She'd never have the nerve . . .

KAREN

Eve would ask Abbott to give her Costello.

LLOYD

No, I got the idea myself — while she was talking to me . . .

KAREN

With gestures, of course.

LLOYD

(wistfully)

For once, to write something and have it realized completely. For once, not to compromise —

Now Karen explodes. She rises.

KAREN

Lloyd Richards, you are not to consider giving that contemptible little worm the part of "Cora"!

LLOYD

Now just a minute ⌐

KAREN

Margo Channing has not been exactly a compromise all these years. Half the playwrights in the world would give their shirts for that particular compromise!

289

LLOYD

(angry)

Now just a minute!

KAREN

It strikes me that Eve's disloyalty and ingratitude
must be contagious!

Lloyd's full of anger and guilt. He snaps back.

LLOYD

All this fuss and hysteria because an impulsive kid
got carried away by excitement and the conniving
of a professional manure slinger named DeWitt!
She apologized, didn't she?

KAREN

On her knees, I have no doubt! Very touching,
very Academy-of-Dramatic-Arts!

LLOYD

That bitter cynicism of yours is something you've
acquired since you left Radcliffe!

KAREN

The cynicism you refer to, I acquired the day I
discovered I was different from little boys!

THE PHONE HAS BEEN RINGING. Lloyd snarls into it.

LLOYD

Hello!

290

(he quiets down)

. . . hi, Margo . . . no, not at all, Karen and I
were just chatting . . . hmm? . . . why — why, yes,
I'm sure we can and I'm sure we'd love to . . .
right . . . 11:45ish. See you then . . .

He hangs up. He smiles — suddenly, there's peace.

LLOYD

Margo — and Bill — want us to meet them at the
Cub Room tonight, after theatre. For a bottle of
wine.

KAREN

(smiles)

Margo in the Cub Room. I couldn't be more surprised if she'd said Grant's Tomb.

LLOYD

I'm glad Bill's back.

KAREN

They'd die without each other.

A pause.

LLOYD

Darling, I didn't promise Eve anything. Just said
I thought she'd be fine for the part, but there
were some practical difficulties . . .

KAREN

Such as?

291

(grins)

You — for one. I told her you were set on Margo playing the part — and that I certainly wouldn't make a change without your approval . . .

Karen smiles happily.

KAREN

That's fine. Fine and dandy. I'd enjoy nothing more. Just refer all of Miss Harrington's future requests to me . . .

DISSOLVE TO:

CUB ROOM — STORK CLUB — NIGHT

Margo, Karen, Bill and Lloyd are ensconced happily at a table in the rear of the room. A bottle of fine wine is being poured. Their mood is equally bubbly.

BILL

The so-called art of acting is not one for which I have a particularly high regard . . .

MARGO

Hear, hear.

BILL

But you may quote me as follows. Quote. To-night Miss Margo Channing gave a performance in your cockamaimy play, the like of which I have never seen before and expect rarely to see again. Unquote.

MARGO

He does not exaggerate. I was good.

BILL

You were great.

As they look at each other, they reflect the understanding
that has hit them both at last.

LLOYD

It's been quite a night. I understand that your
understudy — a Miss Harrington — has given her
notice.

MARGO

(eyes still on Bill)

Too bad.

BILL

(eyes still on Margo)

I'm broken up about it . . .

The wine has been poured by now.

LLOYD

For some reason you can't just pick up champagne
and drink it. Somebody's got to be very witty
about a toast.

(he lifts his glass)

For instance . . .

BILL

(abruptly)

I'm going to propose the toast. Without wit.
With all my heart.

Lloyd lowers his glass. There's a little pause.

BILL

To Margo. To my bride-to-be.

MARGO

Glory hallelujah.

LLOYD

Well of all —

KAREN

Margo!

BILL

Drink.

They drink, then burst into a flurry of questions.

KAREN

When? When are you going to do it?

BILL

Tomorrow we meet at City Hall at ten —
(to Margo)
— and you're going to be on time.

MARGO

Yes, sir.

LLOYD

City Hall, that's for prize fighters, and reporters —
I see a cathedral, a bishop, banks of flowers . . .

BILL

It's only for the license. There's a three-day wait —
blood tests, things like that . . .

MARGO

I'll marry you if it turns out you've got no blood
at all.

KAREN

(to Margo)

What are you going to wear?

MARGO

Something simple. A fur coat over a nightgown.

BILL

The point is — in a cathedral, a ball park or a
penny arcade — we want to have you two beside
us as our nearest and dearest friends . . .

KAREN

. . . which we are. Which we'll always be.

Lloyd fills all the glasses.

LLOYD

There are very few moments in life as good as this.
Let's remember it.

(he lifts his glass)

To each of us and all of us . . . never have we
been more close — may we never be further apart.

They drink. A waiter approaches with a note.

WAITER

Mrs. Richards?

KAREN

Yes?

WAITER

For you.

Karen stares at it curiously, then opens it.

LLOYD

Very indiscreet. A note right out in the open like
that. Next time tell your lover to blow smoke
rings — or tap a glass . . .

MARGO

Lloyd, I want you to be big about this . . . the
world is full of love tonight, no woman is safe.

KAREN

(angrily)

This beats all world's records for running, standing and jumping gall!

She whips the note to Margo, who reads it aloud:

MARGO

(reading)

"Please forgive me for butting into what seems
such a happy occasion — but it's most important
that I speak with you. Please" — it's underlined —
"meet me in the ladies' room. Eve."

296

BILL

I understand she is now the understudy in there.

MARGO

(looking about)

Pass me that empty bottle. I may find her . . .
why, look. There's Rasputin.

THEIR VIEWPOINT

Addison sits near the entrance, at a banquette table for
two. A crumpled napkin and a wine glass indicate Eve's
place. He nibbles daintily at some blini.

THE GROUP

Margo hails a passing captain.

MARGO

Encore du champagne.

CAPTAIN

More champagne, Miss Channing?

MARGO

That's what I said, bub.

LLOYD

(to Karen)

After all, maybe she just wants to apologize.

KAREN

I have no possible interest in anything she'd have
to say.

BILL

But what *could* she say? That's what fascinates me.

LLOYD

Go on — find out.

MARGO

Karen, in all the years of our friendship, I have never let you go to the ladies' room alone. But now I must. I am busting to know what goes on in that feverish little brain waiting in there . . .

KAREN

Well . . . all right.

She gets up and goes. The CAMERA takes her past Addison's table. He rises in polite surprise.

ADDISON

Karen! How nice.

She walks past him without a word. He smiles, looks toward the group. He raises his glass in a toast.

GROUP

Margo responds to the toast by waving an onion with a grand flourish, then eating it.

BILL

Very effective. But why take it out on me?

He eats one in self-defense.

298

Never having been there, I can't say what it looks like. It is to be hoped that there is an outer and inner room. We are concerned with the outer.

There is an attendant in charge, and a constantly changing flow of ladies who pause to make various repairs.

There are two chairs — or a banquette — in a corner. Eve waits there. She rises as Karen approaches.

> EVE
>
> I was wondering whether you'd come at all.

> KAREN
>
> Don't get up.
>> (she smiles grimly)
>
> And don't act as if I were the queen mother.

> EVE
>
> I don't expect you to be pleasant.

> KAREN
>
> I don't intend to be.

> EVE
>
> Can't we sit down? Just for a minute.

She sits. Karen remains standing.

> EVE
>
> I've got a lot to say. And none of it is easy.

299

KAREN

There can't be very much —

EVE

Oh, but there is —

KAREN

— and easy or not, I won't believe a word.

EVE

Why should you?
>   (a pause)
Please sit down.

Karen sits, reluctantly and rigidly.

EVE

You know, I've always considered myself a very
clever girl. Smart. Good head on my shoulders,
that sort of thing, never the wrong word at the
wrong time . . . but then, I'd never met Addison
DeWitt.
>   (another pause)
I remember once I had a tooth pulled. They gave
me some anaesthetic — I don't remember the
name — and it affected me in a strange way. I
heard myself saying things I wasn't even thinking
. . . as if my mind were some place outside of my
body, and couldn't control what I did or said —

300

(leading her on)

— and you felt just like that talking to Addison.

EVE

(nods)

In a way. You find yourself trying to say what you mean, but somehow the words change — and they become his words — and suddenly you're not saying what you mean, but what he means —

KAREN

(sharply)

Do you expect me to believe that you didn't say any of those things — that they were all Addison?

EVE

No! I don't expect you to believe anything. Except that the responsibility is mine. And the disgrace.

KAREN

Let's not get over-dramatic.

EVE

(smiles grimly)

You've really got a low opinion of me, haven't you? Well, I'll give you some pleasant news. I've been told off in no uncertain terms all over town. Miss Channing should be happy to hear that. To know how loyal her friends are — how much more loyal they are than she had a right to expect me to be.

She turns away from Karen. Karen's embarrassed.

> KAREN
>
> Eve . . . don't cry.

> EVE
> (turned away)
> I'm not crying.

> KAREN
>
> Tell me. How did your lunch turn out — with the man from Hollywood?

> EVE
>
> Some vague promises of a test, that's all — if a particular part should come along, one of those things —

> KAREN
>
> But the raves about your performance —

> EVE
>
> — an understudy's performance.

> KAREN
>
> Well. I think you're painting the picture a little blacker than it is, really. If nothing else — and don't underestimate him — you have a powerful friend in Addison.

He's not my friend. You were my friends.

KAREN

He can help you.

EVE

I wish I'd never met him, I'd like him to be dead
. . . I want my friends back.

This time she does cry. Softly, miserably. Karen looks
about. A pause. She puts an arm around Eve.

KAREN

Eve. I — I don't think you meant to cause unhappiness. But you did. More to yourself, perhaps —
as it turned out — than to anyone else.

EVE

I'll never get over it.

KAREN

(smiles)

Yes, you will. You Theatre people always do.
Nothing is forever in the Theatre. Love or hate,
success or failure — whatever it is, it's here, it flares
up and burns hot — and then it's gone.

EVE

I wish I could believe that.

KAREN

Give yourself time. Don't worry too much about

303

what people think. You're very young and very talented . . .

        (she gets up, her hand still on Eve's shoulder)

. . . and, believe it or not, if there's anything I can do —

Eve has reached up to take Karen's hand. She holds it now, as she turns slowly to face her.

EVE

    There is something.

Karen stares down at her. Eve's eyes burn into hers. Karen is caught, fascinated by them.

KAREN

    I think I know . . .

EVE

    Something most important you can do.

KAREN

    You want to play "Cora." You want me to tell Lloyd I think you should play it.

EVE

    If you told him so, he'd give me the part. He said he would.

KAREN

    After all you've said . . . don't you know that part was written for Margo?

                          EVE

It could have been — fifteen years ago. It's my
part, now.

                         KAREN

You talk just as Addison said you did.

                          EVE

"Cora" is my part. You've got to tell Lloyd it's
for me.

                         KAREN

I don't think anything in the world could make
me say that.

She turns away again, but Eve's grip is like a vise.

                          EVE

Addison wants me to play it.

                         KAREN

Over my dead body.

                          EVE

                (cold, relentless)
That won't be necessary. Addison knows how
Margo happened to miss that performance — how
I happened to know she'd miss it in time to call
him and notify every paper in town . . .
            (Karen stops struggling)
. . . it's quite a story. Addison could make quite

                                              305

a thing of it — imagine how snide and vicious he could get and still write nothing but the truth. I had a time persuading him . . .

(she smiles, now)

. . . you'd better sit down. You look a bit wobbly.

(Karen sits)

If I play "Cora," Addison will never tell what happened — in or out of print. A simple exchange of favors. And I'm so happy I can do something for you — at long last.

(Karen covers her face with her hands)

Your friendship with Margo — your deep, close friendship — what would happen to it, do you think, if she knew the cheap trick you'd played on her — for my benefit? And you and Lloyd — how long, even in the Theatre, before people forgot what happened — and trusted you again?

(now Eve gets up)

No . . . it would be so much easier on everyone concerned, if I were to play "Cora." And so much better Theatre, too . . .

Karen looks up slowly.

KAREN

A part in a play. You'd do all that — just for a part in a play.

                        EVE
            (smiles)
      I'd do much more — for a part that good.

She leaves. Karen is alone.

CUB ROOM — NIGHT

Eve enters and slides in beside Addison.

                      ADDISON
      Hungry?

                        EVE
      Just some coffee.

                      ADDISON
            (pours)
      I'm not surprised. After eating so much humble
      pie.

                        EVE
      Nothing of the kind. Karen and I had a nice talk.

                      ADDISON
      Heart to heart? Woman to woman? Including a
      casual reference to the part of "Cora" — and your
      hopes of playing it?

                        EVE
      I discussed it very openly. I told her that I had
      spoken to Lloyd — and that he was interested.

                                              307

ADDISON

She mentioned, of course, that Margo expects to play the part?

EVE

Oddly enough — she didn't say a word about Margo. Just that she'll be happy to do what she can to see that I play the part.

Addison puffs at his cigarette, bemused.

ADDISON

Just like that, eh?

EVE

Just like that.

ADDISON

(thoughtfully)

Do you know, Eve — sometimes I think you keep things from me.

Eve's feelings are hurt.

EVE

I don't think that's funny.

ADDISON

It wasn't meant to be.

EVE

I confide in you and rely on you more than anyone I've ever known! To say a thing like that now

— without any reason — when I need you more
than ever . . .

ADDISON

(breaks in)

I hope you mean what you say, Eve. I intend to
hold you to it.

Their eyes meet.

ADDISON

We have a great deal in common, it seems to me.

They both look up as Karen passes them on her way back
to her table.

GROUP

as Karen joins them. Another bottle of champagne has
come and almost gone — there's a fine, cheery feeling
among them. Margo, in particular, is cheery. A pause.
Karen downs a glass of champagne.

LLOYD

Well? What happened?

KAREN

Nothing much. She apologized.

MARGO

With tears?

KAREN

With tears.

309

MARGO

But not right away? First the business of fighting
them off, chin-up, stout fella . . .

KAREN

Check.

MARGO

Very classy stuff, lots of technique —

LLOYD

You mean — all this time — she's done nothing
but apologize? What'd you say?

KAREN

Not much.

MARGO

Groom —
            (Bill says "Huh?")
— may I have a wedding present?

BILL

What would you like? Texas?

MARGO

I want everybody to shut up about Eve. Just shut
up about Eve, that's all I want. Give Karen more
wine . . .
            (blissfully)
. . . never have I been so happy. Isn't this a lovely

310

room? The Cub Room. What a lovely, clever name. Where the elite meet. Never have I seen so much elite — and all with their eyes on me. Waiting for me to crack that little gnome over the noggin with a bottle. But not tonight. I'm forgiving tonight. Even Eve. I forgive Eve . . . there they go.

They all look.

ADDISON AND EVE

They get up and go without looking back.

GROUP

They watch for an instant.

MARGO

There goes Eve. Eve evil, little Miss Evil. But the evil that men do — how does it go, groom? Something about the good they leave behind — I played it once in rep in Wilkes-Barre . . .

BILL

You've got it backwards. Even for Wilkes-Barre.

MARGO

Do you know why I forgive Eve? Because she left good behind — the four of us, together like this. It's Eve's fault — I forgive her . . .

KAREN'S reactions are, of course, most important. Knowing what she's done to Margo — wondering how to do
what she must.

MARGO

. . . and Bill. Especially Bill. Eve did that, too.

LLOYD

You know, she probably means well after all.

MARGO

She is a louse.

BILL

(to Lloyd)

Never try to outguess Margo.

MARGO

Groom.

BILL

Yes, dear.

MARGO

You know what I'm going to be?

BILL

A cowboy.

MARGO

A married lady.

312

BILL

With a paper to prove it.

MARGO

I'm going to have a home. Not just a house I'm afraid to stay in . . . and a man to go with it. I'll look up at six o'clock — and there he'll be . . . remember, Karen?

KAREN

(quietly)

I remember.

MARGO

(to Bill)

You'll be there, won't you?

BILL

(grins)

Often enough to keep the franchise.

MARGO

A foursquare, upright, downright, forthright married lady . . . that's for me. And no more make believe! Off stage or on . . . remember, Lloyd?

(Lloyd nods)

I mean it, now. Grown-up women only, I might even play a mother — only one child, of course, and not over eight . . .

(they all smile)
Lloyd, will you promise not to be angry with me?

LLOYD

(smiles)
That depends.

MARGO

I mean really, deeply angry.

LLOYD

I don't think I could be.

MARGO

Well. I don't want to play "Cora."

KAREN

(explodes)
What?

Margo misinterprets her vehemence.

MARGO

(hastily)
Now wait a minute, you're always so touchy about his plays, it isn't the part — it's a great part. And a fine play. But not for me any more — not a four-square, upright, downright, forthright married lady . . .

LLOYD

What's your being married got to do with it?

314

MARGO

It means I've finally got a life to live! I don't have
to play parts I'm too old for — just because I've
got nothing to do with my nights!
(then quietly)
I know you've made plans. I'll make it up to you,
believe me. I'll tour a year with this one, anything
— only you do understand — don't you, Lloyd?

Lloyd never gets to answer. Because Karen, before anyone can stop her, is lost in hysterical laughter . . .

LLOYD

What's so funny?

KAREN

Nothing.

BILL

Nothing?

KAREN

Everything . . . everything's so funny . . .

Margo removes the champagne glass from in front of
Karen.

FADE OUT

315

THEATRE — A SILENT SCENE

Karen is seated unobtrusively in a rear lower box. Lloyd sits beside Max up front.

On stage, the play is "on its feet." Eve plays a dramatic scene with a young man. They carry "sides" but do not consult them.

As she speaks, Eve moves upstage, turns to face the young man who is forced to turn his back to the auditorium.

Bill calls a halt. He indicates to Eve that she was to have remained downstage.

Eve seems to be at a loss. She looks at Lloyd.

Lloyd rises, says that he told her to make the change.

Bill comes down to the footlights to tell him to stick to writing, he'll do the directing. It mounts swiftly to a screaming fight. Bill throws the script out into the auditorium, takes his coat and stalks off.

Eve runs after him. Max retrieves the script. Lloyd remains adamant. Karen has risen in dismay.

Eve drags Bill back. Without looking at Lloyd, he takes

316

the script from Max, tells the actors to pick up where they left off.

Eve whispers to Lloyd from the stage. Lloyd smiles, mollified, sits down again with Max.

Karen walks up the side aisle, out of the theatre . . .

> KAREN'S VOICE
>
> Lloyd never got around, somehow — to asking whether it was all right with me for Eve to play "Cora" . . .
>
> Bill, oddly enough, refused to direct the play at first — with Eve in it. Lloyd and Max finally won him over . . . Margo never came to a rehearsal — too much to do around the house, she said. I'd never known Bill and Lloyd to fight as bitterly and often . . . and always over some business for Eve, or a move or the way she read a speech . . . but then I'd never known Lloyd to meddle as much with Bill's directing — as far as it affected Eve, that is . . . somehow, Eve kept them going. Bill stuck it out — and Lloyd seemed happy — and I thought it might be best if I skipped rehearsals from then on . . .

DISSOLVE TO:

317

RICHARDS' BEDROOM — NIGHT

It is a lovely, large room. Two double beds, not alongside each other and each with an extension phone beside it. In addition to the door to the living room, there are two more — to separate dressing rooms and baths.

Lloyd is asleep. But not Karen. She turns restlessly, finally sits up, lights a cigarette.

> KAREN'S VOICE
>
> *It seemed to me I had known always that it would happen — and here it was. I felt helpless, that helplessness you feel when you have no talent to offer — outside of loving your husband. How could I compete? Everything Lloyd loved about me, he had gotten used to long ago . . .*

The phone jangles suddenly, startling her. It wakes Lloyd up. Karen answers.

> KAREN
>
> Hello . . . who? . . . who's calling Mr. Richards?

ROOMING HOUSE — NIGHT

A girl, in a wrapper, at a wall phone. Her hair's in curlers. She's frightened.

> GIRL
>
> My name wouldn't mean anything. I room across the hall from Eve Harrington, and she isn't well.

318

She's been crying all night and hysterical, and she doesn't want a doctor . . .

RICHARDS' BEDROOM

Lloyd is sitting on the edge of the bed, looking over . . .

> LLOYD
>
> Who is it? What's it all about?

> KAREN
> (into phone)
> Did Miss Harrington tell you to call Mr. Richards?

Lloyd picks up his phone.

ROOMING HOUSE

> GIRL
>
> No, Eve didn't say to call him, but I remembered I saw Mr. Richards with her a couple of times — and I thought they being such good friends . . .

RICHARDS' BEDROOM

> LLOYD
> (into phone)
> Hello . . . hello, this is Lloyd Richards. Where is Eve? Let me talk to her —

ROOMING HOUSE

> GIRL
>
> She's up in her room, Mr. Richards. I really hate

to bother you like this, but the way Eve's been feeling — I'm just worried sick what with her leaving for New Haven tomorrow, and everything . . .

RICHARDS' BEDROOM

LLOYD

Tell her not to worry — tell her I'll be right over.

ROOMING HOUSE

GIRL

I'll tell her, Mr. Richards.

She hangs up. As she moves from the phone, the ANGLE WIDENS to disclose Eve at the foot of the stairs. The girls smile at each other. They go upstairs, arm in arm.

RICHARDS' BEDROOM

Karen is still in bed, phone still in her hand. She hangs up, swings her legs out, puts out her cigarette, gets into a robe. The open door and light of his dressing room tell us where Lloyd is.

Karen walks to the door, starts to say something, changes her mind. She crosses to a table, lights a fresh cigarette, comes back to the door.

KAREN

(finally)

Aren't you . . . broadening the duties of a play-

320

wright just a bit? Rushing off in the middle of the night — like a country doctor?

No answer except the opening and closing of drawers.

KAREN

What would you do if, instead of Eve, the leading man had called up to say he was hysterical?

Still no answer. Her tension increasing, Karen goes back to the table, snubs out the fresh cigarette, then strides swiftly back to the open door.

KAREN

Lloyd, I don't want you to go!

Now Lloyd appears. He's in flannels, and a sport shirt with no tie. He's confused and guilty and tortured.

LLOYD

I didn't think you would! It seems to me, Karen, that for some time, now, you've been developing a deep unconcern for the feelings of human beings in general —

KAREN

I'm a human being, I've got some!

LLOYD
(goes right on)

— and for my feelings in particular! For my play,

my career — and now for a frightened, hysterical girl on the eve of her first night in the theatre!

He goes back into his room.

Have you forgotten about Eve? What she is, what she's done?

LLOYD

(from the room)

Old wives' tales, born of envy and jealousy! And a phobia against truth!

KAREN

Then tell me this isn't true! That your concern for your play and career is one thing — and that poor frightened hysterical girl is another — and that your concern for her has nothing to do with either your play or your career!

Lloyd comes out wearing a jacket. He crosses to the door, Karen after him.

KAREN

That first, last and foremost — your reason for going now is that you want to be with Eve! Three in the morning or high noon — play or no play — wife or no wife!

> (Lloyd stops at the door)
> Isn't it true, Lloyd?

Lloyd goes out. Karen looks after him, despairing.

DISSOLVE TO:

SHUBERT THEATRE — NEW HAVEN — DAY

The theatre is but a few doors from the TAFT HOTEL. The marquee announces a new play by Lloyd Richards, presented by Max Fabian, opening tonight.

Addison and Eve stand before the theatre admiring her photo on a lobby display. None of the actors is starred.

> ADDISON'S VOICE
> *To the Theatre world — New Haven, Connecticut, is a short stretch of sidewalk between the Shubert Theatre and the Taft Hotel, surrounded by what looks very much like a small city. It is here that managers have what are called out-of-town openings — which are openings for New Yorkers who want to go out of town.*

They start for the hotel — Eve's arm through Addison's.

CLOSER

as they walk.

323

EVE

What a day — what a heavenly day.

ADDISON

D-day.

EVE

Just like it.

ADDISON

And tomorrow morning, you will have won your beachhead on the shores of Immortality.

EVE

(grins)

Stop rehearsing your column . . . isn't it strange, Addison? I thought I'd be panic-stricken, want to run away or something. Instead, I can't wait for tonight to come. To come and go.

ADDISON

Are you that sure of tomorrow?

EVE

Aren't you?

ADDISON

Frankly — yes.

They've arrived in front of the hotel.

324

EVE

It'll be a night to remember. It'll bring to me everything I've ever wanted. The end of an old road — and the beginning of a new one.

ADDISON

All paved with diamonds and gold?

EVE

You know me better than that.

ADDISON

Paved with what, then?

EVE

Stars.

She goes in. Addison follows her.

DISSOLVE TO:

CORRIDOR — TAFT HOTEL — DAY

Addison accompanies Eve along the corridor to her door.

EVE

What time?

ADDISON

Almost four.

325

EVE

Plenty of time for a nice long nap — we rehearsed most of last night . . .

ADDISON

You could sleep, too, couldn't you?

EVE

Why not?

They've arrived at her door. She opens it.

ADDISON

The mark of a true killer.
              (he holds out his hand)
Sleep tight, rest easy — and come out fighting . . .

EVE

Why'd you call me a killer?

ADDISON

Did I say killer? I meant champion. I get my boxing terms mixed.

He turns to go. After a few steps —

EVE
              (calling)
Addison —
              (he pauses)
— come on in for just a minute, won't you? There's . . . I've got something to tell you.

326

Addison turns curiously, and enters behind her.

EVE'S SUITE — TAFT HOTEL — DAY

Old-fashioned, dreary and small. The action starts in the living room and continues to the bedroom.

Addison closes the door, crosses to a comfortable chair.

> ADDISON
>
> Suites are for expense accounts. Aren't you being extravagant?

> EVE
>
> Max is paying for it. He and Lloyd had a terrific row but Lloyd insisted . . . well. Can I fix you a drink?

She indicates a table elaborately stocked with liquor, glasses, etc. Addison's eyebrows lift.

> ADDISON
>
> Also with the reluctant compliments of Max Fabian?

> EVE
>
> Lloyd. I never have any, and he likes a couple of drinks after we finish — so he sent it up . . .

> ADDISON
>
> Some plain soda.
> (Eve starts to fix it)

327

Lloyd must be expecting a record run in New Haven.

                    EVE
That's for tonight. You're invited. We're having everyone up after the performance.

                  ADDISON
We're?

                    EVE
Lloyd and I.

She carries the soda to him, sits on an ottoman at his feet.

                  ADDISON
I find it odd that Karen isn't here for the opening, don't you?

He sips his soda and puts it away, carefully avoiding a look at Eve. As he looks back —

                    EVE
Addison . . .

                  ADDISON
         (blandly)
She's always been so fanatically devoted to Lloyd. I would imagine that only death or destruction could keep her —

328

EVE
(breaks in)
Addison, just a few minutes ago. When I told you
this would be a night to remember — that it would
bring to me everything I wanted —

ADDISON
(nods)
— something about an old road ending and a new
one starting — paved with stars . . .

EVE
I didn't mean just the theatre.

ADDISON
What else?

Eve gets up, crosses to look out over the Common.

EVE
(her back to him)
Lloyd Richards. He's going to leave Karen. We're
going to be married.

For just a flash, Addison's eyes narrow coldly, viciously.
Then they crinkle into a bland smile.

ADDISON
So that's it. Lloyd. Still just the theatre after
all . . .

329

EVE
(turns, shocked)

It's nothing of the kind! Lloyd loves me, I love him!

ADDISON

I know nothing about Lloyd and his loves — I leave those to Louisa May Alcott. But I do know you . . .

EVE

I'm in love with Lloyd!

ADDISON

Lloyd Richards is commercially the most successful playwright in America —

EVE

You have no right to say such things!

ADDISON

— and artistically, the most promising! Eve dear, this is Addison.

Eve drops her shocked manner like a cape. Her face lights up — she crosses back to the ottoman.

EVE

Addison, won't it be just perfect? Lloyd and I —

there's no telling how far we can go . . . he'll write
great plays for me, I'll make them be great!

      (as she sits)

You're the only one I've told, the only one that
knows except Lloyd and me . . .

ADDISON

. . . and Karen.

EVE

She doesn't know.

ADDISON

She knows enough not to be here.

EVE

But not all of it — not that Lloyd and I are going
to be married . . .

ADDISON

      (thoughtfully)

I see. And when was this unholy alliance joined?

EVE

We decided the night before last, before we came
up here . . .

ADDISON

      (increasingly tense)

Was the setting properly romantic — the lights on
dimmers, gypsy violins off stage?

EVE

The setting wasn't romantic, but Lloyd was. He woke me up at three in the morning, banging on my door — he couldn't sleep, he told me — he'd left Karen, he couldn't go on with the play or anything else until I promised to marry him . . . we sat and talked until it was light. He never went home . . .

ADDISON

You sat and talked until it was light . . .

EVE
(meaningly)
We sat and talked, Addison. I want a run-of-the-play contract.

ADDISON
(quietly)
There never was, there'll never be another like you.

EVE
(happily)
Well, say something — anything! Congratulations, skoal — good work, Eve!

Addison rises slowly, to his full height. As Eve watches him, as her eyes go up to his, her smile fades —

332

ADDISON

(slowly)

What do you take me for?

EVE

(cautiously)

I don't know that I take you for anything . . .

ADDISON

(moving away)

Is it possible — even conceivable — that you've confused me with that gang of backward children you've been playing tricks on? That you have the same contempt for me that you have for them?

EVE

I'm sure you mean something by that, Addison — but I don't know what.

ADDISON

Look closely, Eve, it's time you did. I am Addison DeWitt. I am nobody's fool. Least of all — yours.

EVE

I never intended you to be.

ADDISON

Yes, you did. You still do.

Eve gets up, now.

EVE

I still don't know what you're getting at. Right now I want to take my nap. It's important that I —

ADDISON

(breaks in)
— it's important right now that we talk. Killer to killer.

EVE

(wisely)
Champion to champion.

ADDISON

Not with me, you're no champion. You're stepping way up in class.

EVE

Addison, will you please say what you have to say plainly and distinctly — and then get out so I can take my nap!

ADDISON

Very well, plainly and distinctly. Although I consider it unnecessary — because you know as well as I, what I am about to say . . .

(they are now facing each other)

334

Lloyd may leave Karen, but he will not leave Karen for you.

EVE

What do you mean by that?

ADDISON

More plainly and more distinctly? I have not come to New Haven to see the play, discuss your dreams, or to pull the ivy from the walls of Yale! I have come to tell you that you will not marry Lloyd — or anyone else — because I will not permit it.

EVE

What have you got to do with it?

ADDISON

Everything. Because after tonight, you will belong to me.

EVE

I can't believe my ears . . .

ADDISON

A dull cliché.

EVE

Belong — to you? That sounds medieval — something out of an old melodrama . . .

335

So does the history of the world for the past twenty years. I don't enjoy putting it as bluntly as this, frankly I had hoped that you would, somehow, have known — have taken it for granted that you and I . . .

EVE

. . . taken it for granted? That you and I . . .

She smiles. Then she chuckles, then laughs. A mistake. Addison slaps her sharply across the face.

ADDISON

(quietly)

Remember as long as you live, never to laugh at me. At anything or anyone else — but never at me.

Eve eyes him coldly, goes to the door, throws it open.

EVE

Get out!

Addison walks to the door, closes it.

ADDISON

You're too short for that gesture. Besides, it went out with Mrs. Fiske.

EVE

Then if you won't get out, I'll have you thrown out.

She goes to the phone.

ADDISON

Don't pick it up! Don't even put your hand on it.

She doesn't. Her back is to him. Addison smiles.

ADDISON

Something told you to do as I say, didn't it? That instinct is worth millions, you can't buy it, cherish it, Eve. When that alarm goes off, go to your battle stations.

He comes up behind her. Eve is tense and wary.

ADDISON

Your name is not Eve Harrington. It is Gertrude Slescynski.

EVE

What of it?

ADDISON

It is true that your parents were poor. They still are. And they would like to know how you are — and where. They haven't heard from you for three years . . .

EVE

(curtly)
What of it?

337

She walks away. Addison eyes her keenly.

ADDISON

A matter of opinion. Granted. It is also true that
you worked in a brewery. But life in the brewery
was apparently not as dull as you pictured it. As a
matter of fact it got less and less dull — until your
boss's wife had your boss followed by detectives!

EVE
(whirls on him)
She never proved anything, not a thing!

ADDISON

But the $500 you got to get out of town brought
you straight to New York — didn't it?

Eve turns and runs into the bedroom, slamming the door.
Addison opens it, follows close after her . . . He can be
seen in the bedroom, shouting at Eve who is offscene.

ADDISON

That $500 brought you straight to New York —
didn't it?

BEDROOM

Eve, trapped, in a corner of the room.

EVE
She was a liar, she was a liar!

338

ADDISON

Answer my question! Weren't you paid to get out of town?

Eve throws herself on the bed, face down, bursts into tears. Addison, merciless, moves closer.

ADDISON

There was no Eddie — no pilot — and you've never been married! That was not only a lie, but an insult to dead heroes and to the women who loved them . . .

(Eve, sobbing, puts her hands over her ears. Addison, closer, pulls them away)

San Francisco has no Shubert Theatre, you've never been to San Francisco! That was a stupid lie, easy to expose, not worthy of you . . .

Eve twists to look up at him, her eyes streaming.

EVE

I had to get in, to meet Margo! I had to say something, be somebody, make her like me!

ADDISON

She did like you, she helped and trusted you! You paid her back by trying to take Bill away!

EVE

That's not true!

339

ADDISON

I was there, I saw you and heard you through the
dressing-room door!

Eve turns face down again, sobbing miserably.

ADDISON

You used my name and my column to blackmail
Karen into getting you the part of "Cora" — and
you lied to me about it!

EVE
(into the bed)
No — no — no . . .

ADDISON

I had lunch with Karen not three hours ago. As
always with women who want to find out things,
she told more than she learned . . .
(he lets go of her hands)
. . . do you want to change your story about Lloyd
beating at your door the other night?

Eve covers her face with her hands.

EVE
Please . . . please . . .

Addison gets off the bed, looks down at her.

340

ADDISON

That I should want you at all suddenly strikes me
as the height of improbability. But that, in itself,
is probably the reason. You're an improbable person, Eve, and so am I. We have that in common.
Also a contempt for humanity, an inability to love
or be loved, insatiable ambition — and talent. We
deserve each other. Are you listening to me?

Eve lies listlessly now, her tear-stained cheek against the
coverlet. She nods.

ADDISON

Then say so.

EVE

Yes, Addison.

ADDISON

And you realize — you agree how completely you
belong to me?

EVE

Yes, Addison.

ADDISON

Take your nap, now. And good luck for tonight.

He starts out.

341

EVE

(tonelessly)

I won't play tonight.

(Addison pauses)

I couldn't. Not possibly. I couldn't go on . . .

ADDISON

(smiles)

Couldn't go on? You'll give the performance of your life.

He goes out. The CAMERA REMAINS on Eve's forlorn, tear-stained face. Her eyes close . . . she goes to sleep.

DISSOLVE THROUGH TO:

DINING HALL — SARAH SIDDONS SOCIETY

THE STOPPED ACTION of Eve reaching out for the award. The applause and bulb-popping still going on.

ADDISON'S VOICE

And she gave the performance of her life. And it was a night to remember, that night . . .

THE ACTION picks up where it left off. Eve accepts the award from the aged actor, kisses him tenderly, folds the award to her bosom and waits for quiet.

She speaks with assurance, yet modestly and humbly.

342

Honored members of the Sarah Siddons Society, distinguished guests, ladies and gentlemen: What is there for me to say? Everything wise and witty has long since been said — by minds more mature and talents far greater than mine. For me to thank you as equals would be presumptuous — I am an apprentice in the Theatre and have much to learn from all of you. I can say only that I am proud and happy and that I regard this great honor not so much as an award for what I have achieved, but as a standard to hold against what I have yet to accomplish.

(applause)

And further, I regard it as bestowed upon me only in part. The larger share belongs to my friends in the Theatre — and to the Theatre itself, which has given me all I have. In good conscience, I must give credit where credit is due. To Max Fabian —

MAX

He sits erect, beaming proudly.

EVE'S VOICE

— dear Max. Dear, sentimental, generous, courageous Max Fabian — who took a chance on an unknown, untried, amateur . . .

343

EVE

After applause greets Max.

> EVE
>
> And to my first friend in the Theatre — whose
> kindness and graciousness I shall never forget . . .
> Karen — Mrs. Lloyd Richards . . .

KAREN

Resumes her doodling as applause breaks out for her . . .

> EVE'S VOICE
>
> . . . and it was Karen who first brought me to one
> whom I had always idolized — and who was to
> become my benefactor and champion. A great
> actress and a great woman — Margo Channing.

MARGO

Part of Eve's tribute has been over her CLOSEUP. She
smiles grimly in reaction to the applause.

EVE

She looks to her right, waits for the applause to die.

> EVE
>
> My director — who demanded always a little more
> than my talent could provide —

344

BILL

Seated at the speakers' table. He has his award before him — a smaller one. He puts out a cigarette expressionlessly as the applause breaks out.

> ### EVE'S VOICE
> — but who taught me patiently and well . . . Bill Sampson.

LLOYD

He sits beside Bill. He, too, has a smaller award. As Eve speaks, he throws her a brief glance.

> ### EVE'S VOICE
> And one, without whose great play and faith in me, this night would never have been. How can I repay Lloyd Richards?

EVE

Waits for the applause to die.

> ### EVE
> How can I repay the many others? So many, that I couldn't possibly name them all . . .

ADDISON

He smiles approvingly.

EVE'S VOICE

. . . whose help, guidance and advice have made this, the happiest night of my life, possible.

EVE

She stares at the award for an instant, as if fighting for self-control.

EVE

Although I am going to Hollywood next week to make a film — do not think for a moment that I am leaving you. How could I? For my heart is here in the Theatre — and three thousand miles are too far to be away from one's heart. I'll be back to claim it — and soon. That is, if you want me back.

Another storm of applause. Much ad-lib shouting as Bill and Lloyd are summoned to pose beside her for more pictures. People are thronging out. The aged actor shouts above the hubbub.

AGED ACTOR

A good night to all — and to all a good night!

Eve disengages herself from the photographers, makes her way toward Addison's table . . . Bill and Lloyd follow. CAMERA FOLLOWS Lloyd to Karen. They kiss. He gives her the award.

For services rendered — beyond the whatever-it-is of duty, darling . . .

Max bustles into their SHOT.

Come on! I'm the host, I gotta get home before the guests start stealing the liquor . . .

She and Lloyd follow Max. Addison and Eve are on their way. Lloyd goes right by. Karen pauses by Eve.

Congratulations, Eve.

Thank you, Karen.

Karen goes. Eve is being constantly congratulated. Some ad libs about seeing her at Max's party. Margo and Bill step into the SHOT. Eve turns from a well-wisher to face her.

. . . nice speech, Eve. But I wouldn't worry too much about your heart. You can always put that award where your heart ought to be.

Eve looks at her wordlessly. Margo and Bill leave. Addison and Eve are alone. The tables about them are empty.

Suddenly, her face becomes expressionless, her eyes dull
. . . she glances at the table.

> EVE

I don't suppose there's a drink left . . .

> ADDISON

You can have one at Max's.

> EVE

>> (sits)

I don't think I'm going.

> ADDISON

>> (sighs)

Why not?

> EVE

Because I don't want to.

> ADDISON

>> (patiently)

Max has gone to a great deal of trouble, it's going
to be an elaborate party, and it's for you.

> EVE

No, it's not.

>> (she holds up the award)

It's for this.

ADDISON

It's the same thing, isn't it?

EVE

Exactly.
            (she gives him the award)
Here. Take it to the party instead of me.

ADDISON

You're being childish.

A well-wisher rushes up to Eve with an "Eve, darling,
I'm so happy for you!" Eve rises, thanks her graciously.
Then she pulls her wrap over her shoulder.

EVE

I'm tired. I want to go home.

ADDISON

            (curtly)
Very well. I shall drop you and go on to the party
alone. I have no intention of missing it . . .

They exit from the room, now empty of everything but
tables, waiters and the usual banquet debris.

                              DISSOLVE TO:

PARK AVE — NIGHT

Eve gets out of a taxi in front of a fashionable apartment

349

hotel. She doesn't say good night to Addison, she enters the hotel as the cab drives off. She *hasn't the award* with her.

DISSOLVE TO:

CORRIDOR OUTSIDE EVE'S APARTMENT — NIGHT

Smart, but not gaudy. Eve crosses from the elevator to her apartment. She lets herself in.

EVE'S HOTEL APARTMENT — NIGHT

A small foyer, from which one door leads to the living room, another to the bedroom. The bedroom and living room do not connect except through the foyer.

All the lights are out. Eve turns them on in the foyer, the same as she enters the bedroom. There are some new trunks, in various stages of being packed. Eve tosses her wrap on the bed, goes through the foyer to the living room.

She turns on the lights in the living room. CAMERA FOL-LOWS her to a smart small bar where she fixes a stiff drink.

As she turns from the bar, she stares — starts in fright — and drops the drink.

A young girl, asleep in a chair, wakes with a jump. She stares at Eve, horror-stricken.

350

EVE

Who are you?

GIRL

Miss Harrington . . .

EVE

What are you doing here?

GIRL

I — I guess I fell asleep.

Eve starts for the phone. The girl rises in panic.

GIRL

Please don't have me arrested, please! I didn't
steal anything — you can search me!

EVE

(pauses)
How did you get in here?

GIRL

I hid outside in the hall till the maid came to turn
down your bed. She must've forgot something
and when she went to get it, she left the door
open. I sneaked in and hid till she finished. Then
I just looked around — and pretty soon I was
afraid somebody'd notice the lights were on so I
turned them off — and then I guess, I fell asleep.

351

EVE

You were just looking around . . .

GIRL

That's all.

EVE

What for?

GIRL

You probably won't believe me.

EVE

Probably not.

GIRL

It was for my report.

EVE

What report? To whom?

GIRL

About how you live, what kind of clothes you wear
— what kind of perfume and books — things like
that. You know the Eve Harrington Clubs — that
they've got in most of the girls' high schools?

EVE

I've heard of them.

352

GIRL

Ours was one of the first. Erasmus Hall. I'm the president.

EVE

Erasmus Hall. That's in Brooklyn, isn't it?

GIRL

Lots of actresses came from Brooklyn. Barbara Stanwyck, Susan Hayward — of course, they're just movie stars.

Eve makes no comment. She lies wearily on a couch.

GIRL

You're going to Hollywood — aren't you?
 (Eve murmurs "uh-huh")
From the trunks you're packing, you must be going to stay a long time.

EVE

I might.

GIRL

That spilled drink is going to ruin your carpet.

She crosses to it.

EVE

The maid'll fix it in the morning.

353

I'll just pick up the broken glass . . .

EVE

Don't bother.

The girl puts the broken glass on the bar. She starts to mix Eve a fresh drink.

EVE

How'd you get all the way up here from Brooklyn?

GIRL

Subway.

EVE

How long does it take?

GIRL

With changing and everything, a little over an hour.

She carries the drink over to Eve.

EVE

It's after one now. You won't get home till all hours.

GIRL

(smiles)
I don't care if I never get home . . .

354

The door buzzer sounds.

EVE

That's the door.

GIRL

You rest. I'll get it.

She goes to the door, opens it. Addison stands there, the
Sarah Siddons Award in his hands.

ADDISON

Hello, there. Who are you?

GIRL

(shyly)
Miss Harrington's resting, Mr. DeWitt. She asked
me to see who it is.

ADDISON

We won't disturb her rest. It seems she left her
award in the taxicab. Will you give it to her?

She holds it as if it were the Promised Land. Addison
smiles faintly. He knows that look.

ADDISON

How do you know my name?

GIRL

It's a very famous name, Mr. DeWitt.

355

ADDISON

And what is your name?

GIRL

Phoebe.

ADDISON

Phoebe?

GIRL

(stubbornly)
I call myself Phoebe.

ADDISON

Why not? Tell me, Phoebe, do you want some day
to have an award like that of your own?

Phoebe lifts her eyes to him.

PHOEBE

More than anything else in the world.

Addison pats her shoulder lightly.

ADDISON

Then you must ask Miss Harrington how to get
one. Miss Harrington knows all about it . . .

Phoebe smiles shyly. Addison closes the door. Phoebe
stares down at the award for an instant.

356

EVE'S VOICE
(sleepy — from the living room)
Who was it?

PHOEBE
Just a taxi driver, Miss Harrington. You left the award in his cab and he brought it back.

EVE'S VOICE
Oh. Put it on one of the trunks, will you? I want to pack it . . .

PHOEBE
Sure, Miss Harrington.

She takes the award into the bedroom, sets it on a trunk. As she starts out, she sees Eve's fabulous wrap on the bed. She listens. Then, quietly, she puts on the wrap and picks up the award.

Slowly, she walks to a large three-mirrored cheval. With grace and infinite dignity she holds the award to her, and bows again and again . . . as if to the applause of a multitude.

FADE OUT

About the Author

JOSEPH L. MANKIEWICZ, a native of Wilkes-Barre, Pennsylvania, received his B.A. from Columbia University in 1928 at the age of nineteen. Immediately thereafter he sailed for Europe, ostensibly to continue his studies with a view toward teaching English literature—a destiny more near and dear to the heart of his father, Professor Frank Mankiewicz, than to his own.

Thus the autumn and winter of 1928–29 found Mr. Mankiewicz employed in Berlin, simultaneously translating subtitles of German films being exported to America by the UFA Studios, working as a "stringer" for *Variety* and as an assistant to Sigrid Schultz, chief correspondent for the *Chicago Tribune*.

In March of 1929, at the suggestion of his brother Herman J. Mankiewicz—by then already an eminently successful film scenarist in Hollywood—the younger Mankiewicz left Europe for Southern California. At Paramount Famous-Players Lasky, he signed his first long-term contract with a major film studio.

Over the next twenty-three years Mr. Mankiewicz wrote and/or produced and/or directed films contractually and ceaselessly for Paramount (1929–33), MGM (1933–43) and Twentieth Century-Fox (1943–52). In 1952 he abandoned Southern California as his habitat (an honorable retreat under cover of a barrage of newly won "Oscars") and withdrew to prepared positions in the East.

Together with his wife, Rosemary, and his six-year-old daughter, Alexandra Kate, Mr. Mankiewicz now works and makes his home in Pound Ridge, New York.